PICTURESQUE CHESTER

The City in Art

PICTURESQUE CHESTER

The City in Art

PETER BOUGHTON

PHILLIMORE

1997

Published by
PHILLIMORE & CO. LTD.
Shopwyke Manor Barn, Chichester, West Sussex

ISBN 1 86077 039 8

Printed and bound in Great Britain by
BUTLER & TANNER LTD.
London and Frome

CONTENTS

FOREWORD

BY HIS GRACE THE DUKE OF WESTMINSTER OBE TD DL

The Grosvenor Museum was opened in 1886 by my great-grandfather, the 1st Duke of Westminster. He was also responsible for promoting the black-and-white building revival, which made such a distinctive contribution to Chester's unique character.

The Museum has built a remarkably comprehensive collection of views of Chester through donations and purchases, many grant-aided by the Grosvenor Museum Society, of which I have been President since its establishment in 1980.

Most recently, an imaginative programme of commissions has enabled the Museum to fill many gaps in its collection, as well as showing a refreshing diversity of contemporary artistic responses to the fabric of the city.

Years of essential work on documentation, conservation and research has enabled the production of this book which, through two hundred pictures and an accompanying text, provides a wealth of fascinating information about Chester's architectural history.

Spanning two thousand years of history and four hundred years of art, this book explores the unique heritage of England's most picturesque city. I believe that it will provide great interest and pleasure for residents and visitors alike.

ACKNOWLEDGEMENTS

This book presents the cream of the Grosvenor Museum's comprehensive collection of Chester topography. Over half the pictures reproduced here have been presented to the Museum since its opening in 1886, and thanks are due to the many generous donors. A further quarter of the pictures have been purchased by the Museum since 1952, and we gratefully acknowledge the assistance of grant-aid from the MGC/V&A Purchase Grant Fund, the National Art Collections Fund, the Pilgrim Trust and the Grosvenor Museum Society. Finally, 36 have been commissioned since 1993, and I am grateful to all the artists who have contributed to this programme. The collection has been shaped by generations of curatorial staff, and I particularly wish to thank the Museum's first Keeper of Art, Janet Goose, who created the invaluable topographic index. Most of the pictures in this book have been conserved since 1984 with the assistance of grant-aid from the North West Museums Service—the works of art on paper by Graeme Storey and Nicola Walker and the oil paintings by Harriet Owen Hughes—to all of whom thanks are due.

I am most grateful to His Grace the Duke of Westminster for agreeing to write the foreword to this book. I owe a particular debt of gratitude to Eileen Willshaw, Chester City Council's Heritage Development Manager, who kindly read the draft text and made many helpful comments. Much has already been written about Chester's architectural history, and I am happy to acknowledge my debt to the works listed in the bibliography. I would like to thank Mr. G. Armitage, Oliver Bott, Dr. Peter Carrington, Graham Fisher, Dr. Terry Friedman, Simon Ward and Roy Wilding for much additional information. I also wish to thank Noel Osborne and Nicola Willmot at Phillimore for all their kindness and help. Finally, I am grateful to my colleagues at the Grosvenor Museum, and especially to Simon Warburton, who photographed all the pictures; to Steve Woolfall, Ruth Marshall and Sue Rogers for technical, secretarial and administrative assistance; and to Sharn Matthews, Museums Officer, for her wholehearted support for this project since its inception.

INTRODUCTION

Chester was founded in AD 79 as the Roman fortress of Deva, which became the headquarters of the 20th legion and one of the principal cities of Roman Britain. A civilian settlement grew up outside the Roman fortress whose original defences, a turf bank topped by a timber fence, were rebuilt in stone between 90 and 120. Parts of the Roman masonry remain visible in the north and east walls, most notably a short length of the Roman north wall which still stands to walkway height. The Roman masonry of the Eastgate was discovered when its medieval successor was demolished in 1766, and the principal axes of the city's street pattern follow the layout of the Roman fortress. Just outside the walls lie the remains of Britain's largest stone-built Roman amphitheatre, and the Minerva Shrine, carved into the rock face of a Roman quarry south of the river, is a unique survival.

The Romans abandoned Chester *c.*380. In the fifth and sixth centuries Chester formed part of the Welsh kingdom of Powys, and in the early seventh century it was absorbed into the English kingdom of Mercia. In 689 King Aethelred of Mercia founded St John's Church, and King Offa of Mercia reputedly founded St Bridget's Church in the eighth century. The relics of the Mercian princess St Werburgh were brought to Chester *c.*900 and enshrined in an existing church, dedicated to St Peter and St Paul, on the site of the present cathedral. In 907 Aethelflaed, daughter of King Alfred the Great and wife of Aethelred, ealdorman of Mercia, founded a *burh* or fortified town at Chester. The Roman fortress walls were repaired and possibly extended to the river, and the church of St Peter and St Paul was enlarged and rededicated to St Werburgh. In 1057, on the eve of the Norman Conquest, Leofric, Earl of Mercia, rebuilt St Werburgh's Church and refounded St John's as a collegiate church.

According to tradition King Harold II, wounded rather than killed at the Battle of Hastings in 1066, was brought to Chester and ended his days in the Anchorite's Cell. In 1070 King William the Conqueror came to Chester and established a motte and bailey castle. Its timber structure was soon rebuilt in stone, and the 12th-century Agricola Tower and the Flag Tower on the motte still survive. William also established the County Palatine of Chester, which he granted to his kinsman Hugh Lupus in 1071 and which was governed from Chester Castle. The walls of Chester, the most completely preserved in England, were extended by the Normans to include the castle, with the southern sector being built in the 1120s and the western part *c.*1150-1200. The weir, providing water power for the Dee Mills, is thought to have been constructed under Hugh Lupus.

In 1092 Hugh Lupus refounded St Werburgh's Church as a Benedictine abbey, and a major monastic complex was built from 1092-1220. From this period there remain an arch and triforium in the north transept, the north-west tower, the doorways from the church to the cloisters, and the undercroft. However, the finest Norman church is St John's, which was the cathedral of the diocese of Lichfield from 1075-95. Here, the lowest storey of the nave and chancel plus the crossing and the Lady Chapel arch are Norman, whilst the late 12th-century nave triforium is Transitional. Elsewhere in Chester, St Olave's Church was founded in the late 11th century and the Hospital of St John the Baptist was established *c.*1190.

The earldom of Chester was annexed to the Crown in 1237 and the castle became a royal residence. There were major building works in 1246-53 and 1292-3, particularly in the outer bailey, and fragmentary 14th-century wall paintings survive in the chapel of St Mary de Castro. The Water Tower was built 1322-6 by the mason John de Helpeston to protect Chester's port. The Old Dee Bridge was first built in stone in 1387, replacing a wooden bridge which had existed since at least the early 13th century.

The Rows are unique. They are a system of continuous, covered walkways within the fronts of the buildings at first-floor level. Their origin is unclear, but contributory factors probably include the ruins of the Roman fortress and the shallow bedrock, which kept the cellar floors near to street level. One of the finest of these vaulted stone undercrofts, probably dating from c.1270, is at 12 Bridge Street. Even earlier are the 'Three Old Arches' of c.1200, thought to be Britain's earliest surviving shop front. The Rows system may have been consolidated by widespread rebuilding after a great fire in 1278. Medieval work survives in several of the Row buildings, but one of the best-preserved is Leche House, which has a late 15th-century great hall above an earlier undercroft.

The Early English style is found in the 13th-century nave clerestory and north porch of St John's Church and at St Werburgh's Abbey, beginning with the enlargement of the refectory c.1225-50. The Chapter House was built c.1250-60, and its vestibule is one of the earliest examples in England of piers whose mouldings run into the ribs of the vaulting without intervening capitals. The rebuilding of the abbey church began with the Early English Lady Chapel (c.1260-80). The choir, finished in the early 14th century, was built by the military engineer Richard of Chester. The sandstone shrine of St Werburgh (c.1340) is in the Decorated style. The south transept up to the triforium was built in the mid-14th century, and the south side of the nave was begun c.1360. The magnificent oak choir stalls (c.1380-90) are among the finest in England. Also dating from the 14th century are the Abbey Gateway and the choir chapels of St John's Church.

The basic structure of St Peter's Church dates from the 14th or 15th centuries, and St Mary-on-the-Hill is a Perpendicular church. The remaining medieval work at St Nicholas's Chapel dates from 1488, and the earliest surviving part of St Michael's is the chancel roof of 1496. The south transept of St Werburgh's Abbey was completed in the Perpendicular style, and the north side of the nave was built from 1485-1537, copying the earlier south side in a typically English example of self-conscious conservatism. The west front, unfinished south-west tower and south porch are early 16th century, and the cloisters were rebuilt c.1525-30 in the very last days of the abbey.

In 1538 Chester's three friaries were dissolved, followed in 1540 by St Werburgh's Abbey and St Mary's Nunnery. In 1541 the former abbey church was re-established as a cathedral for the newly-formed diocese of Chester, and the King's School was founded the same year. Following the dissolution of the collegiate church of St John in 1547 it became a parish church, but was shortened on all sides and its east end only survives as ruins. Turning to secular life, organised horse-racing on the Roodee began in 1540. From the early 16th century the chambers above the Rows were often enlarged and had to be supported by posts set in the street, and small shops were later built between the posts at street level. The old County Hall was rebuilt in 1579-81 and Chester's finest Elizabethan house, the timber-framed Stanley Palace, was built in 1591.

By the 17th century some of the Rows were being enclosed, and it also became common for small shops to be erected in them. A Row runs through Bishop Lloyd's Palace (1615), one of Britain's most decorative timber-framed buildings. Chester is renowned for its half-timbered houses, and other fine examples from the early 17th century include Tudor House (c.1603), the Falcon (1626), the Old King's Head and the façade of Leche House. Another prominent feature for many years was the high octagonal water tower built onto the medieval Bridgegate in 1601. At the cathedral, Bishop John Bridgeman created the consistory court (1636) and remodelled the chancel of St Anselm's Chapel. Chester supported King Charles I in the Civil War and suffered a devastating siege from 1644-6. Although the suburbs were initially enclosed within a system of earthen ramparts, they were largely destroyed, and the city walls and the buildings within them were also extensively damaged.

Reconstruction began in the 1650s with buildings such as God's Providence House (1652), Lamb Row (1655) and 1 White Friars (1658). The Dutch Houses, the Nine Houses and Mainwaring House also dated from the mid-17th century. These were all timber-framed, and the Bear and

Billet (1664) is among the last of England's great half-timbered town houses. Later 17th-century buildings included 20 Castle Street (*c*.1680), Harvie's Almshouses (1692) and, most notably, the Exchange (1695-8). Churches also received attention, with the rebuilding of St Bridget's in the mid-17th century and the enlargement of St Michael's in 1678.

The west tower of St Michael's was rebuilt in 1710 and St Martin's Church was rebuilt in 1721. The city walls were repaired as a promenade during the reign of Queen Anne (1702-14), and the tree-lined riverside promenade of the Groves was laid out in 1725. New brick façades were added to the Rows in the 18th century, beginning with Booth Mansion in 1700, and the enclosure of the Rows also continued, as at Tudor House. Fine work of this period includes the façade of Gamul House (*c*.1700), the Bluecoat School (1717) and Dee House (1730). Gun batteries were built at the castle in response to the Jacobite rising in 1745, but the city was not threatened.

Terraced brick housing was built in Abbey Square *c*.1754-61, and the more regular terrace of King's Buildings dates from 1776. The longest and most uniform terrace is in Nicholas Street, built by Joseph Turner in 1781, whilst the grandest house in Georgian Chester was Forest House (*c*.1780). The spire of St Peter's was dismantled *c*.1780, and new churches included the Wesleyan Methodist Octagon Chapel (1765) and Old St Werburgh's Roman Catholic Church (1799). The medieval gates in the city walls were gradually replaced by new ones in the form of bridges to preserve the promenade: the Eastgate was rebuilt in 1768-9, the Bridgegate by Joseph Turner in 1782, and the Watergate in 1788. The Chester Canal was constructed from 1772-9 and Tower Wharf, opened in 1797, retains an important group of canal buildings. Another industrial monument is the 1799 shot tower of Chester Leadworks. Chester Castle, 'the finest group of Greek Revival buildings in Britain' (Howard Colvin), was designed by Thomas Harrison and built from 1788-1815.

The crowning glory of Harrison's castle is the Propylaeum of 1811-5. Harrison's other classical buildings in Chester include the City Club (1807-8), the Northgate (1808-10), Watergate House (1820) and the Grosvenor Bridge (1827-33), once the largest single span stone arch in the world. Harrison also worked in Gothic when refacing medieval buildings at St Peter's Church (1804 & 1811-3), the Agricola Tower (1818) and the cathedral (1818-20). The finest early Gothic Revival building in Chester was the Grosvenor Lodge of 1835 by Thomas Jones. Harrison's pupil William Cole junior designed the Classical St Bridget's Church (1827-8), St Paul's (1829-30) and the Methodist New Connexion Chapel (1835). Chester's Romano-medieval street pattern remained largely unaltered until the 1820s, when Grosvenor Street was cut through diagonally towards the Grosvenor Bridge, causing the demolition of old St Bridget's in 1828. Chester's ancient buildings began to disappear more quickly: the Pentice in 1803, the old Northgate in 1807, the spire of Holy Trinity in 1811, Lamb Row in 1821 and the Shipgate in 1831.

Further losses later in the 19th century included the demolition of Mainwaring House in 1852 and the bishop's palace in 1874, the burning of the Exchange in 1862 and the collapse of St John's tower in 1881. The first railways came to Chester in 1840, and in 1846 a line was cut through the north-west corner of the city walls, but the promenade was preserved with two new bridges. The Water Tower, at that corner of the walls, was opened as a museum in the 1830s, and Chester's cultural life was further enriched with the opening of the Free Library in 1874 and the Grosvenor Museum in 1886. Chester Cemetery (1848-50) is an early example of a park-like burial ground, and Grosvenor Park (1865-7) also retains much of its Victorian character. The Queen's Park Suspension Bridge (1852) leads to the 1850s villa estate of Queen's Park, while the 1860s Albion Street exemplifies working-class housing. The Classical tradition continued fitfully in Victorian Chester, with the enlargement of the Queen Street Congregational Church in 1838, Francis Thompson's Italianate General Railway Station in 1847-8, the Baroque façade of the old Market Hall in 1863, and Michael Gummow's English Presbyterian Church of Wales in 1864.

Although T.M. Penson's Anglican cemetery chapel (1848-50) and east window of St John's (1863) were Neo-Norman, Gothic was the dominant style for ecclesiastical architecture in Victorian Chester, and was also used for some secular buildings. Chester College was built by J.C. & G. Buckler (1841-2) and its chapel by J.E. Gregan (1844-7), while R.C. Hussey undertook major restorations at the cathedral (1843-6 & 1859) and at St John's (1859-66). James Harrison rebuilt St Michael's (1849-50), designed the new Savings Bank (1851-3), adapted St Nicholas's Chapel (1854-5) and St Olave's Church (1858-9), restored St Mary-on-the-Hill (1861-2) and rebuilt Holy Trinity (1865-9). The apogee of High Victorian Gothic is reached with W.H. Lynn's town hall of 1865-9, Sir George Gilbert Scott's thorough restoration of the cathedral in 1868-76 and, on a smaller scale, W. & G. Audsley's Welsh Presbyterian Church of 1866. Late Victorian refinement is exemplified in the work of John Douglas: St Paul's Church (1876), Grosvenor Park Baptist Chapel (1879-80), his restoration of St Peter's Church (1886) and his new bell tower at St John's (1886-7). Other fine examples of late Victorian Gothic include St Werburgh's Roman Catholic Church by Edmund Kirby (1873-5), the King's School by Sir A.W. Blomfield (1875-7) and St Mary-without-the-Walls by F.B. Wade (1886-7).

The black-and-white revival began in Chester in the 1850s with T.M. Penson, whose two shops of 1855 in Eastgate Street are the first new buildings in this style. The revival was strongly promoted by the Chester Archaeological Society, which ensured that when God's Providence House was rebuilt by James Harrison in 1862 it was half-timbered. The early buildings are modest in scale and not very knowledgeable in detail, but this changed when John Douglas and T.M. Lockwood took up half-timbering. Often working for the 1st Duke of Westminster, their black-and-white buildings accurately imitate 16th- and 17th-century motifs, but with greater variety and on a larger scale. The most accomplished practitioner was Douglas, whose earlier buildings include the temporary triumphal arch in City Road (1869), St Werburgh Chambers (1872-3) and the east side of St Werburgh Street (c.1895-7). Douglas also designed a Germanic brick terrace in Grosvenor Park Road (1879-80) and Chester's most famous landmark, the Eastgate Clock (1899). Lockwood's work includes the Plane Tree (c.1873), the corner of Bridge Street and Eastgate Street (1888) and the opposite corner to Watergate Street (1892). Although 95 per cent of the black and white is Victorian and later, it makes as distinctive a contribution to Chester's character as the city walls and the Rows.

John Douglas continued to work throughout the Edwardian era, and his later buildings include parts of Shoemakers' Row (1900) and a terrace of fairytale quaintness in Bath Street (1903). Douglas's pupil James Strong designed another part of Shoemakers' Row (1909) and the former Fire Station (1911), both half-timbered. The finest black-and-white building to be erected since then is the Royal Bank of Scotland by Francis Jones (1921), while Maxwell Ayrton's St Werburgh Row (1935) is built in a rendered vernacular style. Sir Giles Gilbert Scott thoroughly restored the cathedral cloisters and refectory in 1911-3, and a simplified Gothic was used for the sandstone buildings of the hydro-electric power station (1913) and Sir Walter Tapper's Newgate (1938). St Michael's Row by W.T. Lockwood (1910) is faced in white faience, and terracotta appears on the former Westminster Coach Works by P.H. Lockwood (1913-4). Harry Weedon's 1936 Odeon Cinema is a striking Art Deco design, but the new County Hall by E.M. Parkes (1938-57) is bland Neo-Georgian.

The construction of the inner ring road in the 1960s and early 1970s cut a swathe through Chester, affecting mainly 18th- and 19th-century housing, but it enabled the pedestrianisation of the city's historic heart. The depopulation of the city centre led to the redundancy of some churches, but Holy Trinity became the Guildhall in the early 1960s, St Mary-on-the-Hill became St Mary's Centre after 1972, and St Michael's became the Chester Heritage Centre in 1975. Among the best Modern buildings were St Martin's Gate by A.H.F. Jiggens & Grenfell Baines (1966), the Forum by Michael Lyell Associates (1973, but given a Post-Modern façade 1995) and the Addleshaw Tower by George Pace (1975). A small number of high-rise buildings have had a less happy effect upon Chester's skyline. Nevertheless, since 1968 Chester has been in the forefront of architectural conservation in Britain, and many historic buildings and streets have been restored. New buildings have given life to old facades—the former Westminster Coach Works became the Library in 1981-4 and the former Methodist New Connexion Chapel became Habitat in 1984—and the Eastgate Row Development of 1991-3 by Simon Johnson shows great sensitivity to its historic context.

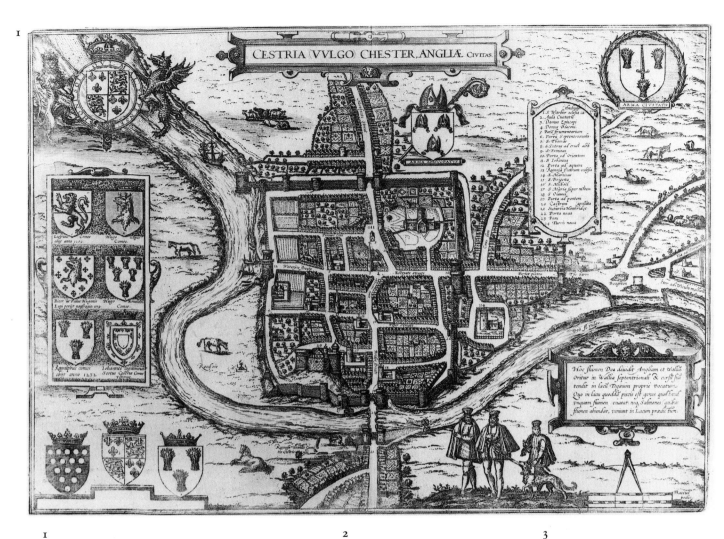

1

GEORG BRAUN (1541-1622) AND
FRANS HOGENBERG (1535-90) AFTER
WILLIAM SMITH (ACTIVE 1568-81)

Plan of Chester in 1581

Engraving 32.4 × 43.7 cm
Presented by E. Gardner Williams
1960.148(99b)

This bird's-eye view of Chester from
the south comes from Braun &
Hogenberg's *Civitates Orbis Terrarum*
('The Cities of the World'), Vol. III
(first published 1581). It shows
shipping on the river Dee, and on the
Roodee a horse and a mound with a
cross, whose shaft still survives. Few
buildings appear along the western
edge of the city within the walls, but
there are large extra-mural develop-
ments to the north, to the south in
Handbridge, and especially to the east.
Further east are the gallows on
Gallows Hill, where the Anglican
priest George Marsh had been
martyred in 1555.

2

ASHBEE & DANGERFIELD
(MID-19TH CENTURY)

*Plan of the Fortifications of
Chester in 1643*

Etching 16 × 19.5 cm
Presented by Edward Davies 1955.506

This plan is a later edition of one
published in Hemingway's *History of
the City of Chester* (1831). The city
supported King Charles I in the Civil
War which began in August 1642, and
the strengthening of Chester's
fortifications commenced the
following month. The outworks,
comprising a system of earthen
ramparts along continental lines, were
completed by the summer of 1643.
They embraced an extensive area to
the north and east of the city walls,
whilst the gate at the Bars (no. 3)
formed an inner defensive bastion and
the river provided natural protection to
the south and west.

3

WILLIAM BATENHAM
(ACTIVE 1813-30) AFTER
WENCESLAUS HOLLAR (1607-77)

Plan of Chester in 1653

Etching 25.9 × 28.3 cm
Presented by Edward Davies 1955.507

Chester was first attacked by Parliamentary forces in July 1643, and the
city was besieged from October 1644
until starved into surrender in
February 1646. The defenders of
Chester destroyed most of the
buildings outside the city walls, and it
is said that within the walls no house
between the Eastgate and the middle
of Watergate Street escaped damage
from Parliamentary bombardment.
Although dated 1653, this prospect
from the west and bird's-eye view from
the south-west appear to show Chester
before the devastation of the siege.
The image is an 1880 reprint of an
1831 copy of Hollar's etching in
Daniel King's *The Vale Royal of England*
(1656).

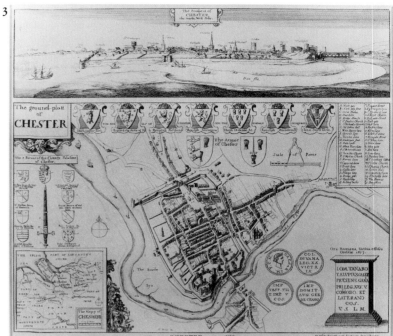

4

PIETER TILLEMANS (1684-1734)

Chester and the Roodee

Oil on canvas 75 × 135.8 cm
Presented by the 1st Duke of Westminster 1965.200

This is the earliest known oil painting of Chester, dating between 1710 and 1734. Viewed from the south-west, it shows horse racing on the Roodee, the course marked by posts and crowds of spectators lining the city walls. The two spires towards the left crowned Holy Trinity Church and St Peter's, and midway between them is the long roof of the Exchange with its central cupola. In the centre of the painting is the cathedral tower, and to the right the castle with the tower of St Michael's behind. Further right is the great west tower of St John's, then the water tower above the Bridgegate, and the Old Dee Bridge.

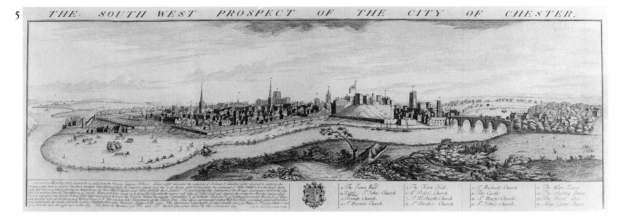

6

5

NATHANIEL BUCK (AFTER 1696-BEFORE 1779) AFTER SAMUEL BUCK (1696-1779)

The South-West Prospect of the City of Chester, 1728

Engraving 26.1 × 71 cm
Purchased 1956.38

Like the painting by Tillemans, this print shows racing on the Roodee. Shipping is depicted on the Dee, whose route to the sea was straightened after 1732, and warehouses are shown near the Watergate and the Water Tower. Other secular buildings within the city walls include the Exchange (5), the castle (10), the water tower above the Bridgegate (13), and the Old Dee Bridge (15) leading to Handbridge on the far right. Most of Chester's churches are also depicted, including Little St John's (2), Holy Trinity (3), St Martin's (4), St Peter's (6), the cathedral (7), St Bridget's (8), St Michael's (9), St Mary-on-the-Hill (11) and St John the Baptist (12).

6

MOSES GRIFFITH (1747-1819)

Chester from Boughton

Pen & ink with watercolour 32.4 × 51.7 cm
Presented by the National Art Collections Fund 1965.183

Painted *c.*1780, this prospect of Chester from the south-east begins at the left with the Old Dee Bridge, the water tower above the Bridgegate and the medieval castle. The two dominant towers in this view belong to St John's and the cathedral, whilst between them are the small tower of St Michael's, the spires of Holy Trinity and St Peter's, and the great block of Forest House. At the far right is the roof of the Octagon Chapel, built by the Wesleyan Methodists at the east end of Foregate Street in 1765 and demolished in the 1860s, and the gallows, which were last used in 1801.

7

UNKNOWN ARTIST (EARLY 19TH CENTURY)

Chester from Boughton

Oil on canvas 45.9 × 61.4 cm
Purchased with grant-aid from the National Art Collections Fund 1958.37

The genteel western suburb of Boughton, favoured as a residential area due to its views over the river, was a popular place from which to paint Chester in the late 18th and early 19th centuries. Although falsely inscribed 'J.S. Cotman 1820', this picture probably dates from *c.*1810. To the left, the broad curve of the Dee flows round the low-lying land known as the Earl's Eye or the Meadows. As in Griffith's depiction of this scene, the skyline is dominated by the towers of St John's and the cathedral, with Forest House between them, but the details are lost in the golden evening light.

7

8

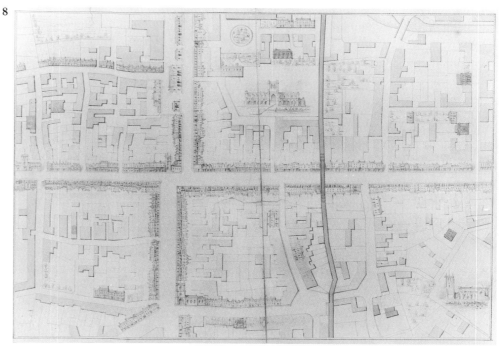

UNKNOWN ARTIST (MID-19TH
CENTURY)

Map of Central Chester

Pencil, pen & ink with grey wash
32.8 × 45 cm
Presented by Ian Catherall Audsley
1995.235

This map was drawn between 1852 and
1858. It illustrates the extent of the
Rows at this date, including the
original Shoemakers' Row in
Northgate Street, and the large
number of buildings with ground-level
arcades in Foregate Street. It also
shows the prevalence of Georgian
brick façades, so many of which were
replaced by the black-and-white revival
later in the 19th century. Several
medieval churches are illustrated,
mostly before their Victorian restorations. In Queen Street, at the top right,
is the Congregational Church, built in
1772 and enlarged in 1838, and to its
left Old St Werburgh's Roman
Catholic Church of 1799.

9

EVANS & GRESTY (ACTIVE 1854-60)

Chester Regatta, 1854

Hand-coloured etching 29 × 38.4 cm
1965.254

Boat races became a well-established
annual feature on the Dee in the 18th
century, when the contests were
entirely between professional boatmen,
but by 1832 there were races for
amateurs as well. The Chester Victoria
Rowing Club was established in 1838
and became the Royal Chester Rowing
Club in 1840, holding an annual June
regatta on the anniversary of Queen
Victoria's coronation. In the distance,
on the riverbank to the right of the
flagpole, is the pumping station of the
Chester Waterworks Company, set up
in 1829 and still supplying the city's
water today.

10

JOHN McGAHEY (ACTIVE *c.*1845-70)

*Aerial View of Chester from the
East, 1855*

Chromolithograph 49.7 × 78.1 cm
Presented by C. Washington 1949.478

In the lower left corner is the Queen's
Park Suspension Bridge. A little
downstream are the snuff mills and
then the Old Dee Bridge, with the Dee
Mills on the right and Handbridge to
the left. Beyond the cemetery and
Grosvenor Bridge are the first villas of
Curzon Park, high above the river
bank. Racing is in progress on the
Roodee, beside which runs the railway
line, with a gasworks beyond. Shipping
lies alongside Crane Wharf and the
Dee Basin is full of canal boats. In the
lower right corner may be seen the
cattle market at Gorse Stacks. Further
along, near the bottom of the picture,
are the Commercial Hall of 1815 to
the east of Frodsham Street and the
Union Hall of 1809 on the south side
of Foregate Street.

11

JOHN FINNIE (1829-1907)

Chester with St John's Church, 1879

Oil on canvas 75 × 120.9 cm
Presented by Mr. Dutton 1957.88

From a low viewpoint on the river bank below Sandy Lane, the artist looks west across the broad curve of the Dee as it flows past the Meadows. He has probably exaggerated the extensive foliage on the north bank of the river, which blends into the trees of the Groves downstream. The row of houses in the centre of the picture is Deva Terrace, behind which rises the great west tower of St John's, whose collapse in 1881 changed Chester's skyline for ever. In the distance, at the left, is the Old Dee Bridge and the silhouette of the castle.

12

BERNARD L. HOWARD

A Prospect of Chester from the North-West, 1995

Watercolour over pencil 36.7 × 54.4 cm
Commissioned 1996.96

At the far left is the Northgate Church in Upper Northgate Street, with its spired turret, built in 1874. To the left of centre is the cupola of the Bluecoat School, followed by the cathedral, Commerce House and the town hall. Commerce House, an office block in Hunter Street, was built in the mid-1960s but was criticised within a few years as an excessively dominant feature of Chester's skyline. At the far right is the even greater bulk of the *Moat House Hotel*, opened in 1988 between Trinity Street and the inner ring road, followed by the spire of the Guildhall.

11

2

II · CHESTER CATHEDRAL

13

DANIEL KING (*c.*1600-65)

South Prospect of the Cathedral, 1656

Etching 19 × 32.6 cm
Presented by E. Gardner Williams
1960.148(17)

During the Dark Ages a wooden church, dedicated to St Peter and St Paul, was built by the Saxons on the site of the present cathedral. The relics of the Mercian princess St Werburgh were brought to Chester *c.*900 to protect the church from Danish raiders and, already credited with miracles, her shrine soon became a focus for prayer and pilgrimage. In 907 Aethelflaed, daughter of King Alfred the Great, enlarged the church and rededicated it to St Werburgh, and in 1057 it was rebuilt by Leofric, Earl of Mercia. The Anglo-Saxon minster was a collegiate church, and its only surviving fragment is two filled-in doorways in the south-east corner of the cloisters.

14

JOHN BUCKLER (1770-1851)

The Cathedral from the South-West, 1811

Watercolour over pencil 45.5 × 65 cm
Presented by the National Art Collections Fund 1965.190

In 1092 Hugh Lupus, Earl of Chester, summoned his friend St Anselm to re-organise the Anglo-Saxon minster into a Benedictine abbey. Between 1092 and 1220 a major monastic complex rose on the old site. The replacement of the Anglo-Saxon minster with the first abbey church began at the east end, just short of the present high altar. The choir and crossing were completed by 1211 and work then began on the nave, reaching to the present west end, but the Norman plans for the abbey remained unfinished. From *c.*1260 to 1537 this Norman abbey church was gradually replaced by the Gothic building we see today.

15

BERTHA GORST (b.1873, ACTIVE 1897-1929)

The Cathedral from the South-West

Etching 17.6 ↔ 25.2 cm
Presented by the Estate of Miss Dandy 1968.88(g)

King Henry VIII dissolved St Werburgh's Abbey in 1540. The following year he re-established the former abbey church as a cathedral, dedicated to Christ and the Blessed Virgin Mary, for the newly-formed diocese of Chester. Although saved from destruction, unlike most English abbeys, all building work stopped at the dissolution. The cathedral was damaged during the Civil War and by the end of the 17th century the whole building was in poor condition. This decay was halted by four 19th-century restorations: by Thomas Harrison in 1818-20, by Richard Charles Hussey in 1843-6, by Sir George Gilbert Scott in 1868-76, and by Sir Arthur William Blomfield in 1882-7.

14

5

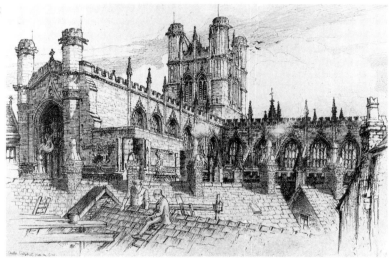

16

16

GEORGE CUITT (1779-1854)

The South Porch, 1810

Etching 25.1 × 26.1 cm
Presented by the Estate of Miss
Dandy 1968.88(l)

The base of the unfinished south-west
tower and the two-storied south porch,
with its highly decorated upper floor,
date from the early 16th century.
Within the porch, the vaulting shafts in
the corners are original, but the fan-
vaulting was constructed by George
Gilbert Scott junior in the late 19th
century. George Cuitt was greatly
influenced by the 18th-century Italian
etcher Giambattista Piranesi. The
architectural details shown here are
accurate but, to heighten the dramatic
impact, the physical decay and the
effect of light and shade have been
exaggerated, and the diminutive figures
give a false sense of grandiose scale.

17

MOSES GRIFFITH (1747-1819)

The South Transept

Pen & ink with watercolour
25.4 × 30.6 cm
Presented by the National Art
Collections Fund 1960.62

Like the Anglo-Saxon minster, the
Benedictine abbey was also a parish
church. The parishioners at first
worshipped in the south aisle of the
nave at an altar dedicated to St Oswald.
When the rebuilding of the nave began
in the mid-14th century they moved to
the nearby chapel of St Nicholas. In
the early 16th century they were given
the south transept as their parish
church. Dedicated to St Oswald, it was
separated from the rest of the
cathedral by a partition at the north
end which remained until 1881, when
St Thomas of Canterbury in Parkgate
Road became the church for the parish
of St Oswald.

18

LOUIS HAGHE (1806-95) AFTER
THOMAS BAILEY (ACTIVE 1828-64)

The Cathedral from the South-East

Lithograph 18.9 × 25 cm
Presented by Scarborough Museum
1953.214

The Lady Chapel was built c.1260-80.
The choir, finished in the early 14th
century, was built by Richard of
Chester, one of the military engineers
responsible for King Edward I's castles
in North Wales. The south transept up
to triforium level was built in the mid-
14th century and later completed in
the Perpendicular style. The monastic
buildings made an extension of the
north transept impossible, so an extra-
large south transept was built to
provide space for more altars. The
south end of the south transept was
rebuilt by Thomas Harrison in 1818-20
with plain stonework and squat corner
turrets.

19

JOSEPH MARTIN KRONHEIM (1810-96)

The Cathedral from the South-East

Lithograph 14.4 × 20.4 cm
Purchased 1958.47

In 1859 Hussey had replaced the east window of the Lady Chapel in the Early English style, and a decade later Sir George Gilbert Scott demolished its south aisle, replaced the southern windows and raised the roof. The south choir aisle now ends in a five-sided apse beneath an absurdly high roof, a feature for which Scott claimed to have found evidence. Scott was also responsible for the Decorated tracery of the windows, and for the flying buttresses, parapets and pinnacles. The four large turrets of the crossing tower are by Scott, but the tall pinnacles between them were removed in 1922.

20

JENNY RYRIE

The Addleshaw Tower, 1996

Pencil, watercolour, conte crayon & acrylic 56.3 × 35.1 cm
Commissioned 1996.101

Bell-ringing in the central tower stopped in 1963 because of structural problems. The solution was to revive the ancient tradition of hanging bells in a free-standing tower, the first to be built for an English cathedral since the Reformation. George Pace began designing in 1968, with calculations of the stresses produced by the change-ringing of 13 bells. The resulting tower, 86 feet high, is of concrete with brick infilling, clad at the base in red sandstone and with small Westmorland slates above. Sited at the south-east corner of the cathedral grounds and opened in 1975, it is named after Dean Addleshaw who commissioned it.

20

21

UNKNOWN ARTIST
(EARLY 19TH CENTURY)

*The Cathedral from Cow Lane
Bridge*

Oil on canvas 58.9 × 71.3 cm
Presented by Mr. & Mrs. S.D. Clarke
1967.628

This view from the north-east is taken beside Cow Lane Bridge, which carries Frodsham Street (formerly called Cow Lane) over the Shropshire Union Canal. The octagonal domed caps on the turrets at the east end of the choir date from the 17th or 18th centuries, and the battlements on the turrets of the central tower were probably added by Thomas Harrison. The cathedral is constructed of the local red sandstone, which weathers very badly. As a result, most of the exterior was refaced during the Victorian restorations which began in 1843, although much genuine medieval masonry remains inside.

22

ROBERT LINNELL ARMITAGE
(b.1898, ACTIVE 1931)

*The West Front and the King's
School*

Etching 17.5 × 29.6 cm
Bequeathed by Councillor S.H.M.
Lloyd 1989.105

The bishop's palace was demolished in 1874. The bishops moved to a Georgian house overlooking the Groves, and since 1921 the bishop's house has been the former deanery in Abbey Square. In 1875-7 the site next to the cathedral was rebuilt as the King's School by Sir Arthur William Blomfield. The school had been founded by Henry VIII in 1541, and from the early 17th century was housed in the cathedral refectory. In 1960 a new school opened in Wrexham Road, and the building beside the cathedral is now occupied by Barclay's Bank.

23

23

GEORGE CUITT (1779-1854)

The West Front, 1811

Etching 24.8 × 25.5 cm
Presented by E. Gardner Williams
1960.148(113)

The west front dates from the early
16th century but was later restored and
embellished by Scott. The sculpture
above the west door, which is flanked
by canopied niches, culminates in the
Assumption of the Virgin, and a huge
eight-light Perpendicular window rises
above. The Norman north-west tower
has always been hidden by a building,
so nearly one-third of the façade is
missing. This building was originally
the abbot's lodging. In 1541 it became
the bishop's palace, which was
remodelled by Sir Robert Taylor for
Bishop Edmund Keene in 1754-7.

24

Thomas Bailey (active 1828-64)

The Entrance to the Consistory Court, 1849

Watercolour over pencil 30.9 × 23.5 cm
Presented by T. Cann Hughes 1925.8

In 1636 the ground floor of the unfinished south-west tower was turned into the consistory court. The oak furnishings and the stone screen that separates it from the aisle were given by Bishop John Bridgeman. This picture depicts the east side of the screen, with its typically early 17th-century cresting. The springer in the corner above the screen shows that the medieval builders had intended to construct a vault, but an open timber roof had been built instead: the nave aisles had to wait for Scott's restoration before they received their stone vaults.

25

William Monk (1863-1937)

The Consistory Court, 1890

Etching 15.7 × 25 cm
Presented by E. Gardner Williams 1960.148(1c)

The consistory court is the court of the bishop, and its judge is the chancellor of the diocese. Chester has the only complete example in England of an old consistory courtroom, comprising a wooden enclosure with a bench around a large table. Over the canopy of the chancellor's throne appear the arms of Bishop Bridgeman, Hugh Lupus, the Chester Diocese and Chancellor Edmund Mainwaring. An ecclesiastical court was last convened here in the 1930s.

25

THE CONSISTORY COURT

26

MOSES GRIFFITH (1747-1819)

The Interior of the Nave

Pen & ink with grey wash over pencil
34.9 × 39 cm
Presented by the National Art
Collections Fund 1960.63

This view is taken from the south nave
aisle, through the nave and the
crossing, to the north transept. Work
on the south side of the nave began
*c.*1360, and the north side was built
from 1485-1537, copying the earlier
work in a typically English example of
self-conscious conservatism. Towards
the centre of this picture can be seen
part of the *pulpitum*, the medieval stone
screen which divided the choir from
the nave: sections of this were later re-
set by Scott in the north and south
choir aisles.

26

27

J. LEWIS STANT (ACTIVE 1931-9)

*The Interior of the North
Transept*

Colour etching 30.1 × 21.2 cm
Presented by Mrs. B.M. Gough
1967.626

The arch and triforium in the east wall
belonged to the north transept of the
Norman abbey church. They date
from the end of the 11th century and
are the oldest part of the cathedral. To
the east of this arch is a former chapel,
originally with an apse but rebuilt with
a straight end *c.*1200. Between this arch
and the choir aisle is a piscina, a basin
for washing the mass vessels, and the
fragment of masonry to its right may
have belonged to a screen. The
transept's splendid roof of 1518-24 is
the oldest timber roof in the cathedral.

27

28

CHARLES JOSEPH HULLMANDEL
(1789-1850) AFTER JOHN SKINNER
PROUT (1806-76)

The Bishop's Throne, 1838

Lithograph 27.2 × 17.3 cm
Purchased 1977.92

The sandstone shrine of St Werburgh,
dating from *c*.1340, held the chest
containing her relics. Its original
location is uncertain, but from the
Reformation until Scott's restoration it
stood in the choir and formed the base
of the bishop's throne. The wooden
panelling and canopy seen here were
probably installed by Bishop
Bridgeman in the early 17th century.
When Hussey restored the choir in
1843-6 he raised the band of tracery to
form a high canopy, adding slender
pinnacles and gilding the statuettes.
Since 1889 the shrine has stood at the
west end of the Lady Chapel, where it
was restored by Blomfield.

29

ALLEN EDWARD EVERITT (1824-82)

*The Bishop's Throne and Choir
Stalls*

Watercolour over pencil 34.6 × 48.5 cm
Purchased 1969.38

The magnificent oak choir stalls,
among the finest in England, date
from *c*.1380-90. Above the seats are
high, spiky, closely set canopies with
crocketed arches and spirelets. The
ends of the seats are carved with
poppy heads, and the arm rests are
carved as well. The greatest array of
carving is on the 48 *misericords*, the
small ledges on the undersides of the
tip-up seats which supported the
monks during long periods of
standing. As this picture shows,
Hussey moved the medieval stone
choir screen and wooden choir stalls
one bay further west beneath the
crossing tower.

28

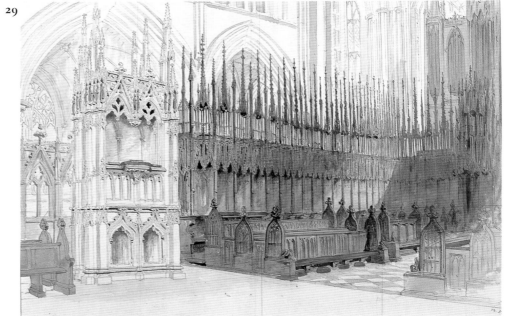

30

AUGUSTUS OSBORNE LAMPLOUGH
(1877-1930)

*The Organ and Choir Screen,
1898*

Watercolour over pencil 49.4 ↔ 30.9 cm
Purchased 1969.11

Scott moved the choir stalls back one
bay east to their original position and
replaced the solid stone choir screen
with an open wooden one. The centre
of Scott's screen originally housed a
small set of organ pipes, but these
were replaced by a carved Crucifixion
in 1913. Behind the hanging cross may
be seen Scott's rib-vaulted ceiling with
painted decoration by Clayton & Bell.
On the left of the crossing is the organ
loft and case, which forms a splendid
terminus to the vista from the south
transept and is probably Scott's finest
work in the cathedral.

Organ and Choir Screen
Chester
Cathedral

31

BERTHA GORST (b.1873, ACTIVE 1897-1929)

Interior of the Choir

Etching 12 × 7.9 cm
Purchased 1993.3

The magnificent pair of bronze sanctuary candlesticks, given in 1872, were made in early 17th-century Rome by the bronze-founder Orazio Censore. Scott's delicate wrought-iron altar rails were replaced in 1965 with modern ones designed by George Pace, who adapted some of the panels for St Erasmus's Chapel in the south choir aisle. The large metal cross hanging above the choir screen had been made to Scott's design by Francis A. Skidmore of Coventry, but was transferred to the church at Dunham-on-the-Hill in 1921. Beyond the cross is the timber lierne-vault with which Scott replaced the nave's open roof.

32

W. CRANE (ACTIVE *c.*1831-4) AFTER MOSES GRIFFITH (1747-1819)

The Vestibule to the Chapter House

Lithograph 15.4 × 17.5 cm
Presented by E. Gardner Williams 1960.148(14)

Chester's monastic buildings, on the north side of the cathedral, are among the best preserved in Britain. Following the Rule of St Benedict, the monks worshipped eight times a day in the abbey church, and they studied, cared for the sick, welcomed travellers and fed the poor. This beautifully proportioned vestibule leads from the east cloister to the chapter house, and the cathedral clergy and choir assemble here before services. The 13th-century vestibule is architecturally important as one of the earliest examples in England of piers whose mouldings run into the ribs of the vaulting without any intervening capitals.

33

W. CRANE (ACTIVE *c.*1831-4) AFTER MOSES GRIFFITH (1747-1819)

The Chapter House

Lithograph 19.1 × 13.5 cm
Presented by E. Gardner Williams 1960.148(15)

The chapter house was where the monks listened to a daily chapter from the Rule of St Benedict. It was also the burial place of the abbots and for most of the Norman earls of Chester. The dean and chapter now meet here monthly to discuss cathedral business. Built *c.*1250-60, the chapter house was described by Nikolaus Pevsner as 'the aesthetic climax of the cathedral, a wonderfully noble room'. Between the slender lancet windows are boldly detached shafts with rings, rising to stiff-leaf capitals. The east window was filled with stained glass in 1872 and the Georgian panelling has been removed.

34

THOMAS BAILEY (ACTIVE 1828-64)

Door to the East Cloister, 1849

Watercolour over pencil 26.9 × 22.7 cm
Presented by T. Cann Hughes 1925.4

At the heart of Chester's monastic
buildings are the cloisters, four arcaded
walks around a central garden. Here

the monks could sit to read and write
at desks in alcoves called *carrells*. The
cloisters were originally laid out when
the first abbey church was built in the
12th century, and the wall of the south
cloister still contains Norman work.
This picture shows the major doorway
from the church to the cloister, which
is the cathedral's finest example of late
Norman architecture.

35

GEORGE CUITT (1779-1854)

The North Cloister looking East,
1811

Etching 25.1 × 26.2 cm
Presented by the Estate of Miss
Dandy 1968.71

The cloisters were largely rebuilt
*c.*1525-30, in the very last days of the
abbey, with rib-vaults and Perpendicular windows. The north cloister adjoins
the refectory, and the long stone shelf
in the north wall was the *lavatorium.*
Here the monks washed before meals,
probably from a stone or lead trough
containing the water. The semi-derelict
window to the right has been used by
George Cuitt to dramatic effect,
framing a view which sweeps diagonally across the cloister garden and up
to the central tower.

36

ALFRED BENNETT BAMFORD
(1857-1939)

The Cloister Garth, 1883

Watercolour 25.5 × 15.9 cm
Presented by Chester College of
Further Education 1965.173

The cloisters lost their religious
function after the dissolution of the
monastery. The south cloister was
demolished and the others fell into
decay, with much of the Perpendicular
tracery disappearing from the
windows. This picture shows the
north-west corner of the cloisters
before their restoration. In the
background to the right is the
refectory, and to the left are two
cottages built for lay clerks of the
cathedral in 1626.

37

ALFRED BENNETT BAMFORD
(1857-1939)

The Cloister Garth, 1936

Watercolour over pencil 34 × 22.5 cm
Presented by Chester College of
Further Education 1965.177

Sir Giles Gilbert Scott undertook a
thorough restoration in 1911-3, which
included rebuilding the demolished
south cloister. In 1921-7 the windows
were filled with beautiful stained glass
depicting the saints of the Anglican
calendar. This picture shows the north-
east corner of the cloisters with the
refectory in the background. In the
foreground is the cloister garden,
which was laid out in the 1920s. The
fountain in the middle of the garden
occupies the site of the abbey's
reservoir, which was fed by a piped
water supply from the village of
Christleton three miles away.

38

WILLIAM MONK (1863-1937)

The Refectory Pulpit, 1890

Etching 25 × 15.7 cm
Presented by E. Gardner Williams
1960.148(1b)

The refectory was the monastic dining
hall, where the 30 or 40 monks ate
their single daily meal. The structure is
basically Norman, although it was
enlarged in the Early English style
*c.*1225-50. The triangular projecting
stone pulpit, from which one of the
monks read aloud during mealtimes, is
approached by a flight of steps set into
the thickness of the wall. The
refectory survived the dissolution by
becoming the King's School. It was
restored by Sir Giles Gilbert Scott in
1911-3, and the hammer-beam roof
was designed by Frederick H. Crossley
in 1939.

39
ROBERT KENT THOMAS (1816-84)
AFTER GEORGINA F. JACKSON
(ACTIVE 1878-93)

The Undercroft

Lithograph 24.7 × 37.3 cm
Presented by Sir Wyndham Dunstan
1942.292

The undercroft beside the west cloister
was probably used for storage. Built
*c.*1140 in the Norman style, it is groin-
vaulted in two aisles divided by short
round piers with scalloped capitals. It
escaped later rebuilding because the
abbot's lodging was above, but by the
16th century soil from the adjacent
abbot's garden had built up inside and
it was no longer used. The undercroft
was excavated and restored in 1849,
but served as the cathedral workshop
until the northern half became a
bookshop in 1977 and the rest an
exhibition area in 1992.

40

40
WILLIAM MONK (1863-1937)

St Anselm's Chapel, 1890

Etching 24.9 × 15.8 cm
Presented by E. Gardner Williams
1960.148(1f)

Dating from the 12th century, this was
the private chapel for the adjoining
abbot's lodging, which subsequently
became the bishop's palace. The
chancel bay, which extends over the
cloister walk, was remodelled in the
early 17th century by Bishop
Bridgeman for his own use. He gave
the fine stucco ceiling, the carved
wooden screen and the altar rails. The
ceiling of the rest of the chapel is a
19th-century Gothic plaster vault.

41

41

WILLIAM BATENHAM (ACTIVE 1813-30)

Abbey Square

Grey wash over pencil 8.9 × 12.8 cm
Presented by J.H. Chandler 1975.168(i)

Abbey Square was originally the outer courtyard, around which were various buildings used in the abbey's administration. Today there is a central green surrounded by cobbled paving. The south side of the square, on the right of this picture, was the site of the abbot's lodging, which became the bishop's palace. On the east side of the square, to the left of the picture, are the stone cottages built for the lay clerks of the cathedral by Bishop Bridgeman in 1626. On the north and west sides are terraces of brick houses built *c*.1754-61.

42

ARTHUR GODWIN (1900-89)

Abbey Gateway, 1931

Etching 12.5 × 8.7 cm
Presented by the Estate of Miss Dandy 1968.88(d)

The abbey gateway leads from the west side of Abbey Square into Northgate Street. Built in the 14th century, the vaulted roof of the gateway has carved bosses. The upper floor with its Gothic window was rebuilt in the late 18th or early 19th century.

42

43

43

UNKNOWN ARTIST (MID-19TH
CENTURY)

St John's from the North-East

Watercolour over pencil 24.3 × 37.8 cm
Presented by T. Cann Hughes 1925.22

The church of St John the Baptist was
founded by King Aethelred of Mercia
in 689 and was refounded as a
collegiate church in 1057 by Leofric,
Earl of Mercia. Bishop Peter of
Lichfield transferred his see to Chester
in 1075 but his successor removed it to
Coventry in 1095. During the intervening twenty years St John's Church was
the cathedral of the diocese, and is
said to have retained the status of a
cathedral, with Lichfield and Coventry,
until the new diocese of Chester was
formed in 1541.

44

44

WILLIAM GILLARD (*c.*1812-97)

St John's from the East

Oil on canvas 37.3 × 29.7 cm
Presented by Thomas Ellis 1965.198

St John's Church was collegiate, and at
the time of its dissolution in 1547 was
served by a dean, seven canons and
four minor canons. After the dissolution it became a parish church and
parts of the building fell out of use.
The east end of the chancel, the Lady
Chapel and the choir chapels now only
survive as ruins, whilst the transepts
and nave have been shortened. The
church is built of soft red sandstone,
which weathers very badly, and parts
of the exterior were restored in the
18th century. The house beside the
north porch was demolished in 1855.

45

UNKNOWN ARTIST (MID-19TH
CENTURY)

*The Tower and West End of
St John's from the South*

Watercolour 23.7 × 18.1 cm
Purchased 1958.106

The external appearance of the church
today is largely a Victorian version of
Early English Gothic. This is partly
due to Richard Charles Hussey, who
restored the south side and the west
end, together with the interior, in
1859-66. Hussey remodelled the aisle
windows, rebuilt the aisle roof with a
steeper pitch, crowned the west gable
with a cross and flanked it with turrets.
He also decorated the exterior of the
clerestory with an arcade to match that
which already existed on the interior,
thereby greatly enriching what had
previously been unadorned masonry.

45

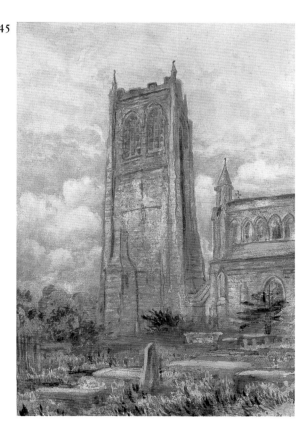

46

Unknown Artist (active 1881)

St John's Tower after its Collapse, 1881

Oil on canvas 25 × 34.8 cm
Purchased with grant-aid from the
MGC/V&A Purchase Grant Fund
1989.145

The 16th-century upper part of the west tower collapsed on Good Friday 1881, changing Chester's skyline for ever. The rector described 'a rumbling noise, which was succeeded by a terribly and indescribably long drawn-out crash, or rather rattle, as though a troop of horse artillery was galloping over an iron road; this was mingled with a clash of bells, and when it had increased to a horrible and almost unbearable degree, it suddenly ceased, and was succeeded by perfect stillness.' It proved impossible to raise the money to rebuild the tower, and only the ruins of the 12th-century base remain.

47

Unknown Artist
(late 19th century)

St John's in Winter

Lithograph 16.9 × 23.2 cm
Presented by E. Gardner Williams
1960.148(82a)

The collapse of the west tower destroyed the Early English north porch, which John Douglas rebuilt with the old stones in 1881-2. In 1886-7 he built a new bell tower at the north-east corner of the church. The tower's main feature is its Germanic roof, which is a two-tier pyramid with two projecting clock faces having their own hipped roofs, whilst the bells hang in a wooden framework beneath the eaves. In 1887 Douglas restored the north side of the church at the Duke of Westminster's expense, following the model of Hussey's earlier restoration of the south side.

48

GEORGE CUITT (1779-1854)

The East End of St John's, 1811

Etching 24.7 × 25.6 cm
Presented by E. Gardner Williams
1960.148(114)

The present east wall was constructed
in 1581 when the building was
shortened to make it more suitable for
use as a parish church. The large east
window lit the chancel and the small
one to the left was for the south aisle.
The tracery of both windows
incorporated earlier stonework,
reassembled in imitation of 14th-
century Gothic. The south aisle
window still survives, although
blocked, but the chancel window was
replaced with an ungainly Neo-
Norman design by Thomas
Mainwaring Penson in 1863.

49

GEORGE CUITT (1779-1854)

The Ruins of St John's

Etching 24.2 × 25.4 cm
Presented by E. Gardner Williams
1960.148(33)

To the east of the present church are
medieval ruins—a subject much
favoured by early 19th-century British
artists. The dissolution of the college
in 1547 made this part of the church
redundant, and the east end fell into
ruins. This view from the east shows
the Norman arch to the Lady Chapel,
beyond which was the probable site of
the medieval high altar. To either side
of this arch are the remains of the
14th-century choir chapels, whilst the
small Gothic canopy lying beneath the
arch once formed the head of a niche.

50

CORNELIUS VARLEY (1781-1873)

The Nave of St John's, 1802

Watercolour over pencil 33.1 × 24.3 cm
Purchased with grant-aid from the
V&A Purchase Grant Fund and the
Grosvenor Museum Society 1985.99

The lowest storey of the nave and
chancel is Norman, and has round
piers with many-scalloped capitals and
double-stepped arches. Although the
Norman building may have been
begun before 1095 the work remained
incomplete. The late 12th-century nave
triforium is Transitional, with four
pointed arches on ringed shafts in each
bay. The 13th-century nave clerestory
is Early English, also with four arches
per bay, the shafts with leaf capitals
and the windows alternating with
blank arches. Vaulting shafts rise from
the triforium floor level, but the vault
was never built.

50

51

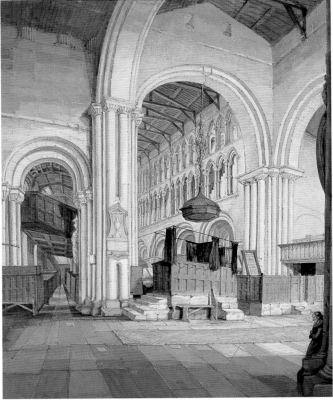

51

UNKNOWN ARTIST, MONOGRAM J.M.
(EARLY 19TH CENTURY)

The Interior of St John's

Watercolour & bodycolour over pencil
33.4 × 28 cm
Purchased 1972.164

Since the late 16th century the interior
of the church has comprised a four-
bay nave (originally three bays longer),
a splendid Norman crossing—seen
here—and the first bay of the Norman
chancel, plus one surviving bay of
each transept. In the 18th century the
nave was fitted with box pews, galleries
were installed down the aisles and
across the west end, and a sounding
board on an elaborate wrought-iron
support was suspended above the
pulpit. The interior was whitewashed
in 1788, which may be the wall surface
shown here. The Georgian fittings
were removed in Hussey's restoration
of 1859-66.

52

Alfred Bennett Bamford
(1857-1939)

The Lady Chapel, St John's

Watercolour over pencil 33 × 23.5 cm
Presented by Chester College of
Further Education 1965.176

The east end of the south aisle is now
the Lady Chapel. It is entered through
massive 17th-century oak gates with
very rich wrought-iron railings and
finials. The oak reredos, with

Corinthian pilasters and swan-necked
pediments, is formed from two
sections of the former high altar
reredos of 1692. It was transferred
here *c.*1876-7, and it was probably at
this time that the two arched panels
were fitted with paintings of the
Annunciation. The early 18th century-
style altar rails date from *c.*1925, but
the paintings were removed in 1969
when an aluminium figure of the
Blessed Virgin Mary by Michael
Murray was installed.

53

53

JOHN VARLEY (1778-1842)

Lamb Row and St Bridget's, 1803

Watercolour 21.5 × 30 cm
Presented by Alderman E. Peter Jones
1940.271

Reputedly founded by King Offa of
Mercia in the eighth century, St
Bridget's is first certainly recorded in
1200. The church originally stood on

the corner of White Friars and Bridge
Street, opposite St Michael's. Rebuilt in
the mid-17th century, it was re-cased
externally with stone in 1785 when the
surrounding churchyard was removed.
Behind Lamb Row, in the centre of
this picture, can be seen the tower of
St Bridget's and beyond it the east end
of the church. St Bridget's was
demolished in 1828 to make way for
Grosvenor Street.

54

LOUIS HAGHE (1806-95) AFTER
GEORGE PICKERING (1794-1857)

St Bridget's and the Castle

Lithograph 19.4 × 24.8 cm
Purchased 1979.19

A new St Bridget's Church was built on
the corner of Nicholas Street and
Grosvenor Street. Thomas Harrison
made several Greek cross designs in
1820 and a more modest series in 1826.
Some of Harrison's ideas were then
adapted by his pupil William Cole
junior, to whose design the church was
built in 1827-8. This elegant Neo-
Classical building, harmonising with
Harrison's nearby Castle, had Greek
Doric pilasters supporting a pediment
at the west end and a cupola with Ionic
columns above. In 1891 St Mary-on-
the-Hill became the parish church for
St Bridget's, which was demolished the
following year.

54

55

GEORGE BATENHAM (ACTIVE FROM 1794, d.1833)

St Martin's Church

Etching 10.6 × 15 cm
Purchased 1993.70

The medieval parish of St Martin was one of the smallest in Chester. The church, which stood on the east side of Nicholas Street, dated from the 13th century. It had become ruinous by 1721, and was then rebuilt in brick with stone details at a cost of £187. In 1842 the parish of St Martin was united with that of St Bridget, and by the 1870s the church was used for Welsh services. In 1964 the building was bought by Chester City Council and demolished to make way for the inner ring road.

56

ALFRED BENNET BAMFORD (1857-1939)

St Mary-on-the-Hill

Watercolour over pencil 32.6 × 23.7 cm
Presented by Chester College of Further Education 1965.182

Standing on the top of St Mary's Hill, this church is of Norman foundation although its appearance today is Perpendicular. Built of red sandstone, much of the external masonry is Victorian, but the lower part of the west tower has a much weathered early 16th-century doorway. The church was restored by James Harrison in 1861-2 and again by John Pollard Seddon in 1890-1. Harrison added 30 feet to the tower, but the tops of the pinnacles have since been removed. Following redundancy in 1972 the church was purchased by Cheshire County Council, and as St Mary's Centre it is now used for meetings and exhibitions.

57

Unknown Artist (active 1849)

St Michael's Church, 1849

Oil on wood 75 × 59.8 cm
Purchased with grant-aid from the
V&A Purchase Grant Fund and the
Trustee Savings Bank 1976.137

Rebuilt after a fire in 1180, the oldest
part of the present church is the
chancel roof, dating from 1496. St
Michael's was enlarged in 1678 and the
west tower, beneath which passes
Bridge Street Row East, was rebuilt in
1710. This picture shows the church
immediately prior to 1849-50, when it
was largely rebuilt by James Harrison.
Following redundancy in 1972 St
Michael's was purchased by Chester
City Council and reopened in 1975 as
Chester Heritage Centre, Britain's first
architectural heritage centre. Remodelled in 1991, its displays explore the
development of Chester's unique
townscape.

58

58

Michelle-Anne Williams

*St Nicholas's Chapel and
St Werburgh Row, 1994*

Watercolour with pen & ink over
pencil 41.4 × 59.1 cm
Commissioned 1994.10

The chapel of St Nicholas is said to
have been built early in the 14th
century, and the parishioners of St
Oswald's moved here a little later. The
remaining medieval work probably
dates from an enlargement in 1488.
From 1545-1698 it was used by the
Corporation as the Common Hall,
before being converted into the Wool
Hall. In use as a playhouse by 1727, it
became the Theatre Royal in 1777. In
1854-5 James Harrison adapted the
building as the Music Hall and
designed its Tudor Gothic façade to St
Werburgh Street. It became a cinema
in the 20th century and is now a shop.
The adjacent St Werburgh Row was
built in 1935 by Maxwell Ayrton.

59

Isobel Messer

St Olave's Church, 1994

Pastel over watercolour & bodycolour
52.1 × 23.7 cm
Commissioned 1994.36

St Olave's Church in Lower Bridge
Street is a small sandstone building
with a bell cote at its west end. St
Olave was King Olaf of Norway, who
helped establish Norwegian Christian-
ity before his death in 1030. The
church was founded later in the 11th
century, possibly to serve a small
community of traders from the Norse
settlement of Dublin. The church and
its parish were always the smallest and
poorest in Chester, and in 1841 the
church was closed and the parish
united with St Michael's. In 1858-9
James Harrison restored the building
as the parochial Sunday School, and it
later became an adult education centre.

59

60

THOMAS WEBSTER (1772-1844)

St Peter's from Bridge Street

Pencil with grey wash 31.5 × 49 cm
Presented by Lieutenant Colonel
Norrie 1961.92

St Peter's Church at the Cross was
traditionally founded in 907 by
Aethelflaed, daughter of King Alfred
the Great, and is mentioned in
Domesday Book of 1086. Internally,
the basic structure is of the 14th or
15th centuries, but the church has been
altered and restored several times
since. The spire was dismantled *c.*1780
after having been struck by lightning.
Along the south wall of the church
was the Pentice, a timber-framed
building with shops at ground level
and the Corporation's administrative
headquarters above. At its west end,
over the steps and porch leading into
St Peter's, stood the rector's two-storey
house.

61

AFTER JOHN DOUGLAS (1830-1911)

St Peter's Church, 1887

Lithograph 22 × 28 cm
Presented by E. Gardner Williams
1960.148(36a)

The Pentice was removed in 1803, and
Thomas Harrison refaced the south
side of St Peter's in 1804 and the tower
in 1811-3. The church was restored by
John Douglas in 1886. He changed the
tracery of the upper windows on the
south side to the Perpendicular style
and added square-headed windows
below: there are two tiers of windows
because Douglas kept the north and
south galleries. He also gave the tower
its low, two-tiered pyramidal roof,
which completes the view of the
church from Bridge Street. This
picture shows a passage beneath the
east end and an elaborate door
surround which were not executed.

60

61

62

GEORGE BATENHAM (ACTIVE FROM
1794, d.1833)

Holy Trinity Church

Etching 12.6 × 17.7 cm
Purchased 1993.71

Holy Trinity Church, on the corner of
Watergate Street and Trinity Street, is
first recorded in 1188. The medieval
church on this site was altered in the
17th and 18th centuries. Its dilapidated
spire was dismantled in 1811, on
Thomas Harrison's advice, and the
tower given a square top. The church
was originally built up to the pavement
of Watergate Street, rather than having
the small forecourt we see today.

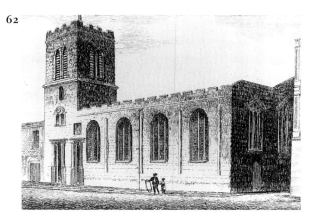

62

63

LOUISE RAYNER (1832-1924)

*Watergate Street and Holy Trinity
Church*

Watercolour with bodycolour
27.4 × 12.9 cm
Presented by Miss B. Cann Hughes
1950.715

Holy Trinity was virtually rebuilt in
1865-9. It was designed by James
Harrison and completed after his
death by Kelly & Edwards. Built of red
sandstone in the Decorated Gothic
style, its most prominent feature is the
fine south-west steeple. The old tower
was reinforced so that a new spire
could be erected on it, and this
terminates the vista up from the
Watergate. A new church dedicated to
the Holy Trinity was built further out
in the parish at Blacon, and since the
early 1960s the old Holy Trinity
Church has been used as the Guildhall.

63

64

J. Sadler (late 19th century)

The Anchorite's Cell

Oil on card 30.1 × 48.7 cm
Presented by Mrs. O. Price 1976.448

This little sandstone building is perched on an outcrop of rock in the former quarry, now laid out as a bowling green, between St John's Church and the Groves. According to local tradition, King Harold II, merely wounded rather than killed at the Battle of Hastings in 1066, was brought to Chester by his friends and ended his days in this cell as a hermit. Known as the Anchorite's Cell or the Hermitage, the medieval building was restored as a house in the 19th century, probably using stonework from St John's.

64

65

Neale T. Evans

The Bluecoat School, Upper Northgate Street, 1994

Watercolour over pencil 29.5 × 46.3 cm
Commissioned 1994.43

The Hospital of St John the Baptist was founded on this site by Earl Ranulph III of Chester (1181-1232) for 13 'poor and feeble men'. The hospital survived the Reformation but its buildings were pulled down by the defenders of Chester during the Civil War siege. The Bluecoat School was built in 1717 to house a charity school founded by Bishop Nicholas Stratford of Chester in 1700. The left wing of this building was occupied by the hospital's chapel, known as St John the Baptist without the Northgate or Little St John. The almshouses behind the school were rebuilt in 1854, but the school closed in 1949 and the chapel followed in the 1960s.

65

66

RONALD BASIL EMSLEY WOODHOUSE
(b.1897, ACTIVE 1924-32)

*Chester College Chapel, Parkgate
Road*

Etching 24.8 × 35.1 cm
Purchased 1994.1

Chester College was established in
1839 as a Church of England teacher
training college. The first building,
designed by John Chessell Buckler and
George Buckler in the Tudor style, was
erected in 1841-2. The chapel,
designed by J.E. Gregan of Manchester, was built in 1844-7 of rock-
faced red sandstone in the Decorated
style. It was partly constructed, and the
fittings almost entirely made, by the
college students, who were taught
manual labour and crafts. The college
has expanded considerably since the
Second World War and is now known
as University College Chester.

67

RICHARD HORE

St. Paul's Church, Boughton, 1994

Watercolour & bodycolour over pencil
53.5 × 36.8 cm
Commissioned 1994.37

St Paul's had been built in 1829-30 by
William Cole junior in the Classical
style, but this was rebuilt by John
Douglas in 1876. The roof sweeps
down in one pitch over both nave and
aisles, and a huge three-sided apse
extends their full width. Douglas had
recently remodelled Whitegate Church
in Cheshire, where parts of the
medieval timber-framing survived, and
this inspired his use of wood at St
Paul's, where the internal structure is
entirely of timber. The charming Arts
and Crafts painted wall decoration
probably dates from 1902, when
Douglas added a south aisle.

66

68

ALISTER WINTER ROBERTS

Bath Street and St Werburgh's Church, 1994

Watercolour over pencil 38.1 × 56 cm
Commissioned 1995.2

St Werburgh's Roman Catholic Church in Grosvenor Park Road replaced Old St Werburgh's Church in Queen Street, which had been built in 1799. The new church, built in 1873-5, was designed in the Early English style by Edmund Kirby of Liverpool, a pupil of John Douglas. It was originally intended to have a spire 200 feet high, but this was never built due to lack of money. Indeed, the west end with its apse and chapels—seen here—was not completed until 1913-4. The adjacent terrace in Bath Street, with bulging conical-roofed turrets of fairytale quaintness, was built by John Douglas in 1903.

68

69

ALISTER WINTER ROBERTS

Grosvenor Park Baptist Chapel, 1994

Watercolour over pencil 38.3 × 56 cm
Commissioned 1995.3

The chapel was designed by John Douglas and built in 1879-80. The gable end has three windows with late 13th-century style geometrical tracery. There are stone wall shafts between these windows, and brick wall shafts beneath them with pairs of tiny lancets. Flanking the gable end are square turrets rising to octagonal Germanic roofs with massive lead finials, whilst a slender spire originally rose from the centre of the roof. Douglas's adjacent brick terrace complements the chapel with its steep roofs, many gables, and octagonal turrets at either end.

70

JENNY RYRIE

The Methodist New Connexion Chapel, Pepper Street, 1994

Pencil, watercolour, conte crayon & acrylic 53.3 × 74.7 cm
Commissioned 1995.1

The Methodist New Connexion Chapel, designed by William Cole junior and built in 1835, was the most impressive Classical nonconformist chapel in Chester. Its rich and boldly modelled façade, with a deep Corinthian portico beneath a heavy attic, contrasts with the same architect's chaste Grecian design for St Bridget's of the previous decade. The chapel closed just after the First World War, and in the 1930s the building was incorporated into an extensive motor showroom which concealed the facade. It was revealed again in 1984 and restored as the centrepiece of a Habitat superstore.

69

70

71

MARGARET HUGHES

*The English Presbyterian Church 71
of Wales, City Road, 1994*

Watercolour over pencil 38 × 55.9 cm
Commissioned 1994.29

Chester lies very close to the border
with Wales, and the Welsh have long
made up a sizeable proportion of the
city's population. This chapel in City
Road was one of several for Welsh
nonconformists. It was built in 1864 as
the Welsh Calvinistic Methodist
Chapel and became Presbyterian in the
20th century. Designed by Michael
Gummow of Wrexham, its stuccoed
Classical façade is reminiscent of the
Methodist New Connexion Chapel in
Pepper Street, but the Greek Ionic
columns and the omission of the attic
give it a lighter feel. The original cast-
iron gates survive, but the railings
between them are modern.

71

72

JULIA MIDGLEY

*The Welsh Presbyterian Church,
St John Street, 1994*

Watercolour & bodycolour over pencil
38 × 52.5 cm
Commissioned 1994.35

The Welsh Presbyterian Church was
designed by W. & G. Audsley of
Liverpool and built in 1866. The body
of the church is of brick, whilst its
façade is of stone with contrasting
textures. The style is Early English but
treated with High Victorian vigour, an
enormous rose window rising
dramatically above the projecting
three-bay porch. It is one of the two
remaining churches in Chester where
services are still held in Welsh,
although there had been several others,
including St Martin's, before the
Second World War.

72

73

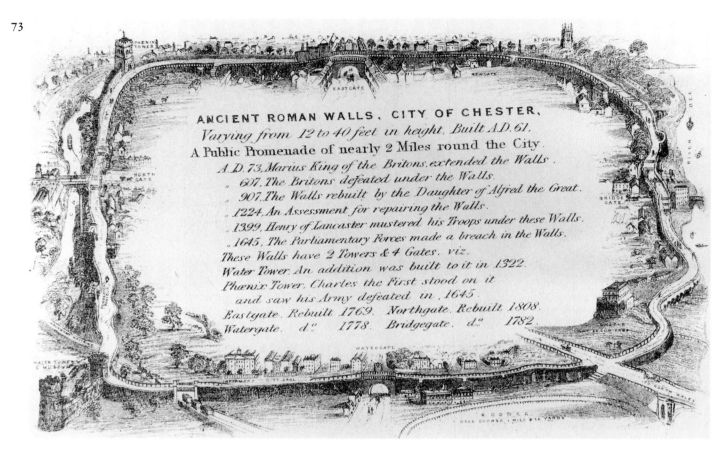

ANCIENT ROMAN WALLS, CITY OF CHESTER,
Varying from 12 to 40 feet in height, Built A.D. 61.
A Public Promenade of nearly 2 Miles round the City.
A.D. 73, Marius King of the Britons, extended the Walls.
" 607, The Britons defeated under the Walls.
" 907, The Walls rebuilt by the Daughter of Alfred the Great.
" 1224, An Assessment for repairing the Walls.
" 1399, Henry of Lancaster mustered his Troops under these Walls.
" 1645, The Parliamentary Forces made a breach in the Walls.
These Walls have 2 Towers & 4 Gates, viz.
Water Tower. An addition was built to it in 1322.
Phœnix Tower. Charles the First stood on it
and saw his Army defeated in 1645.
Eastgate. Rebuilt 1769. Northgate. Rebuilt 1808.
Watergate. d°. 1778. Bridgegate. d°. 1782.

73

EVANS & GRESTY (ACTIVE 1854-60)

Bird's Eye View of the City Walls

Engraving 7.8 × 12.3 cm
Presented by Mrs Bradbury 1973.32(c)

Chester's walls were first built when the Roman fortress of Deva was founded AD 79. Deva was the Roman army's base for controlling the troublesome tribes of North Wales and northern England, and the 20th legion was posted to Deva, which became a permanent fortress and legionary headquarters. The first Roman defences were made up of a turf bank topped by a timber fence, but between 90 and 120 they rebuilt the gates, towers and walls in stone.

A facing of massive sandstone blocks was built against the front of the turf bank, and some parts are still visible in the east and north walls. The Roman army left in the late fourth century, and in the ninth and 10th centuries Chester became an important base in the wars between Saxons and Vikings. In 907 it was re-fortified by Aethelflaed, the daughter of King Alfred, but no identifiable remains of the Saxon wall are visible today. In the early 12th century the Normans extended the walls to the south and west to include the castle. These new walls were free-standing, unlike the old Roman ones. New watch-towers were added, and the main gates had a drawbridge and portcullis.

74

UNKNOWN ARTIST
(LATE 19TH CENTURY)

The King Charles Tower and the North Wall from the Canal

Etching 13.3 × 19.5 cm
Purchased 1954.247

Chester was loyal to King Charles I during the Civil War, and the city was besieged for 18 months from 1644-6 by the Parliamentary forces. Their guns bombarded the defences, causing great damage to the walls, before the city was starved into surrender. The walls remained in ruins until the reign of Queen Anne (1702-14), when they were repaired, although little attempt was made to preserve the medieval details. With peace and increasing prosperity the walls, no longer needed for defence, became instead a pleasant promenade, and the medieval gates were gradually replaced by new ones in the form of bridges to preserve the walls walk. In the 20th century new gates have been built to take increased traffic, and today the city walls are a scheduled ancient monument owned by Chester City Council.

74

75

JOHN MUSGROVE (ACTIVE 1810-31)
AFTER JAMES CALVELEY (ACTIVE
1774-91)

The Roman Eastgate

Coloured lithograph 33.6 × 30.6 cm
Presented by Alderman E. Peter Jones
1943.330(27)

Four massive gateways guarded the
entrances to the Roman fortress of
Deva. Most important was the east
gate, the Porta Principalis Sinistra,
opening onto the main road to
London and York. The double Roman
arch illustrated here was discovered
when the medieval Eastgate was
demolished in 1766. The passageway
through the medieval Eastgate had
incorporated the Roman arches on the
right, while those to the left were
concealed in the tower at the side. The
carved figure between the arches was
described as a soldier or Mars, the
Roman god of war, and above the
gateway was an inscription to the
emperor carved on Welsh slate.

GEORGE BATENHAM (ACTIVE FROM
1794, d.1833) AFTER GEORGE
WILKINSON (ACTIVE 1781-95)

The Medieval Eastgate

Etching & aquatint 15.5 × 12.2 cm
Presented by John Stuffins 1954.408

The medieval Eastgate was similar in
style to the early 14th-century King's
Gate at Caernarfon Castle. It was taken
down in 1766, and illustrations made at
about that time show that it was a
pointed archway between two
octagonal towers four storeys high, the
whole structure topped by battlements.
Like most of the city gates, the
Eastgate was held not by the Corporation but by individuals from the Earl
of Chester. These included the earls of
Oxford and the Crewe family, who
employed gate-keepers and charged
tolls on all goods passing through.

BERTHA GORST
(b.1873, ACTIVE 1897-1929)

The Eastgate from Foregate Street

Etching 18.8 × 25 cm
Purchased 1993.1

As in most other English walled towns
and cities, Chester's medieval gates
were demolished in the late 18th and
early 19th centuries to ease the flow of
traffic. In Chester, the gaps in the
circuit were bridged in order to
preserve the promenade, but these
bridges were still called 'gates'. The
oldest is the Eastgate, rebuilt in 1768-9
by a Mr. Hayden at the expense of
Richard, Lord Grosvenor. It has a
rusticated elliptical arch, the keystone
carved with the City arms on the
Foregate Street side and the Grosvenor
arms facing Eastgate Street. Small,
round-arched openings provide
pedestrian passages to either side.

RICHARD HORE

The Eastgate Clock, 1996

Bodycolour over pencil 76 × 56 cm
Commissioned 1996.97

The clock turret spanning the walkway
over the centre of the Eastgate arch
was erected in 1899. It was designed by
John Douglas and commemorates
Queen Victoria's Diamond Jubilee of
1897. Decorated with the date, royal
monogram, roses and crowns, this
fanciful confection has a suitably
festive character. The open wrought-
iron structure was made by Douglas's
cousin, James Swindley of
Handbridge. The clock is by J.B. Joyce
of Whitchurch, and until 1974 was
wound by hand once a week. The
Eastgate Clock has become Chester's
most famous landmark, and is said to
be the most photographed clock in the
world after Big Ben.

79

W. WHITE (MID-19TH CENTURY)

The King Charles Tower from the Canal

Oil on canvas 74.9 × 62.1 cm
Purchased with grant-aid from the
Grosvenor Museum Society 1988.72

The King Charles Tower is the north-east corner tower of both the Roman and medieval defences. It still retains some of its medieval appearance, although it has been restored several times. On 24 September 1645 King Charles I stood on this tower while his army was being defeated by the Parliamentarians on Rowton Moor, about two miles to the south-east. What he actually saw was not the battle itself but the scattered remnants of his army being pursued through the suburbs. The king later moved to the cathedral tower, where he was narrowly missed by a bullet fired from St John's Church.

80

80

JOHN GRESTY (ACTIVE 1850-82)

The King Charles Tower from the Walls

Chromolithograph 29 × 19.2 cm
Purchased 1977.51

The King Charles Tower is said to have been known at an early date as Newton's Tower, but by the 17th century it was called the Phoenix Tower. In the Middle Ages many watch towers were used as meeting places for the city guilds. Above the doorway is a plaque carved in 1613, which marks the use of this tower by the Painters, Glaziers, Embroiderers and Stationers Company, whose emblem was a phoenix. The King Charles Tower is now a small museum about the Civil War in Cheshire.

81

JOHN GODFREY (*c*.1817-89) AFTER
HENRY WARREN (1794-1879)

The King Charles Tower from the Walls

Engraving 15.5 × 18.7 cm
Purchased 1979.14

Some of the most spectacular discoveries relating to Roman Chester were made when the section of the north wall from the King Charles Tower to St Martin's Gate was repaired in the 1880s and 1890s. About 150 Roman tombstones, most of them inscribed to the memory of soldiers of the 2nd or 20th legions, had been used to reinforce the inside of the wall in the 3rd century AD. The stones are now housed in the Grosvenor Museum. Towards the Northgate a short length of the Roman fortress wall still stands to walkway height. This dates from *c*.90-120, when the Romans built a stone wall in front of the turf bank.

81

MOSES GRIFFITH (1747-1819)

The Medieval Northgate

Pen & ink with watercolour
31.3 × 29.4 cm
Presented by Miss Margaret S. Davies
1962.99

The Roman Northgate, the Porta
Decumana, was on this site. The
medieval gate was defended by towers,
a portcullis, and a drawbridge which
crossed the outlying town ditch. The
Chester Canal, begun in 1772, runs in a
dramatic deep cutting which follows
the line of the ditch. Inside and below
the medieval Northgate was the
infamous city gaol. Used until 1807,
both gate and gaol were under the
control of the city sheriffs. Parts of
the gaol were excavated from the rock
below the wall and included 'The Dead
Men's Room', where men who were
condemned to death were confined.

83

GEORGE BATENHAM (ACTIVE FROM
1794, d.1833) AFTER JAMES HUNTER
(ACTIVE 1781-1822)

The Medieval Northgate, 1808

Etching & aquatint 12.7 × 19.3 cm
Presented by E. Gardner Williams
1960.148(19)

On the right is Little St John's Chapel
in the south wing of the Bluecoat
School, which was built in 1717. In
1793 this was linked to the medieval
Northgate by a narrow stone foot-
bridge over the canal, known as the
Bridge of Sighs. According to
tradition, condemned felons were led
across this bridge from the Northgate
gaol to receive their last rites in the
chapel.

84

GEORGE BATENHAM (ACTIVE FROM 1794, d.1833)

The Northgate, 1815

Etching 25 × 39.2 cm
Presented by Miss Estelle Dyke
1963.36(b)

The Northgate was rebuilt in 1808-10 at the expense of the 2nd Earl Grosvenor, who was Mayor of Chester in 1807-8. It was designed by Thomas Harrison in the austere Neo-Classical style. Built of finely cut grey Runcorn sandstone, the deeply coffered segmental arch is flanked by pedestrian passages between pairs of baseless, unfluted Doric columns. The solid parapets, bearing inscriptions, give it a more sombre appearance than Chester's 18th-century gates.

84

85

THOMAS BAILEY (ACTIVE 1828-64)

Morgan's Mount

Pen & ink 7.8 × 11.8 cm
Purchased 1954.253(a)

The watch-tower called Morgan's Mount has a lower chamber at the level of the wall, with steps leading to an open platform above. It is named after a Captain Morgan who, according to legend, commanded a Royalist gun mount at the foot of the wall here during the siege of Chester in the Civil War. At this time the walls were repaired and strengthened, and gun batteries and cannon were moved into position. They were especially important around the north-western ramparts with their commanding views and considerable strategic value.

85

86

87

86

BERNARD L. HOWARD

St Martin's Gate, 1993

Watercolour over pencil 49.2 × 72.9 cm
Commissioned 1993.76

St Martin's Gate, the newest of
Chester's gateways, was built to keep
the walls circuit intact after the inner
ring road was constructed. It was
opened in 1966 by Mrs. Barbara Castle,
the Minister of Transport. The gate
was designed by A.H.F. Jiggens, the
City Engineer, and Grenfell Baines of
the Building Design Partnership. It is
an elegant example of 1960s design,
combining simplicity and lightness.
The site of the north-west corner
tower of the Roman wall is marked in
the pavement to the right.

87

THOMAS BAILEY (ACTIVE 1828-64)

Pemberton's Parlour

Pencil 17.7 × 24.4 cm
Presented by Alderman E. Peter Jones
1943.330(32)

Pemberton's Parlour is the remnant of
a defensive tower formerly known as
Dill's or the Goblin Tower. The
original medieval tower was a much
taller, circular building, which straddled
the walls and had a central passageway
for pedestrians. It was badly damaged
by Parliamentarian cannon in 1645. In
the reign of Queen Anne the south
side of the tower was demolished and
the north side converted into an alcove
with seats. It was reconstructed again
in 1894. The Parlour is named after
John Pemberton, Mayor of Chester in
1730-1, who owned a ropewalk
beneath the wall and supervised his
men from this tower.

88

THOMAS ALLOM (1804-72)

*The City Walls, with Pemberton's
Parlour*

Sepia & blue wash over pencil
9.8 × 15.7 cm
Presented by the National Art
Collections Fund 1965.206

The Corporation officials responsible
for keeping the walls in repair were the
Murengers, two of whom were elected
each year. They collected a special tax
called murage (from *murus*, the Latin
for wall) which was levied on certain
goods coming into the port of
Chester. An inscription on
Pemberton's Parlour records the
names of the Murengers and the
Mayors from 1702-8. Visible from this
stretch of the wall is the panorama of
the Clwydian Hills, of which the
highest is Moel Famau ('the mother of
hills'). Its summit is crowned with the
Jubilee Tower, designed by Thomas
Harrison and built in 1810-*c*.1815.

89   90

FRANCIS NICHOLSON (1753-1844)

*Bonewaldesthorne's Tower and the
Water Tower*

Watercolour 17.4 × 26.3 cm
Purchased 1967.1

The rectangular Bonewaldesthorne's
Tower stands at the north-west angle
of the medieval walls. From the 12th
to the 14th centuries, when Chester
was a busy port, this tower guarded the
harbour and shipping moored beside
the walls. By the early 14th century
extensive silting had caused the river
Dee to change course away from the
base of Bonewaldesthorne's Tower, so
the New or Water Tower was built
further out in the Dee, connected by a
100-foot-long spur wall. The tower
cost £100 and was built in 1322-*c.*1326
by the mason John de Helpeston, who
was also employed at Flint Castle.

90

THOMAS BAILEY (ACTIVE 1828-64)

Interior of the Water Tower, 1837

Pencil 25.8 × 21 cm
Presented by Alderman E. Peter Jones
1943.330(48)

The river originally flowed up to the
Water Tower, but only one hundred
years later silt had once again choked
the river channel and water ceased to
reach the tower, which now stands on
dry land. The Water Tower is about 75
feet high, and its walls at the lower
level are about 12 feet thick. The lower
chamber, seen here, is a vaulted
octagon, with moulded ribs springing
from the angles of the walls and an
arrow-loop at the end of each deep
recess. The upper room, also octagonal, is reached by a spiral stair.

91

91

J.W. WALSHAW (ACTIVE FROM 1892, d.1906)

Bonewaldesthorne's Tower

Watercolour 26.3 × 20.2 cm
Presented by T. Cann Hughes 1925.10

A stairway descends from the wall to what are now the Water Tower Gardens. The path passes through an arch in the spur wall, which bears an inscription recording that it was rebuilt in 1730 during the mayoralty of John Pemberton. The niche near Bonewaldesthorne's Tower contained a statue of Queen Anne, which came from the south face of the Exchange after it burned down in 1862, but which vanished in the 1960s.

92

EVANS & GRESTY (ACTIVE 1854-60)

The Water Tower and the Railway

Engraving 8.3 × 11.1 cm
Presented by Mrs. Bradbury 1973.32(a)

In 1846 the railway line from Chester to Ruabon was cut through two sections of the wall at its north-west corner, but the wall walk was carefully preserved with new bridges. The tracks still carry all trains between Chester and North Wales. The Water Tower had been taken over as a museum by the Chester Mechanics Institution in the 1830s, and a camera obscura, which has now been restored, was installed on the roof of Bonewaldesthorne's Tower. The towers are now one of the Chester Museums.

92

93

94

95

George Batenham (active from 1794, d.1833) after George Wilkinson (active 1781-95)

The Medieval Bridgegate

Etching & aquatint 16.3 × 11.1 cm
Presented by A.O. Orrett 1963.54(1)

Standing at the city end of the Old Dee Bridge, the medieval Bridgegate guarded the only approach to Chester from Wales and was therefore known as the Welshgate. The custody of the Bridgegate was shared between the Norrises, who sold their portion to the Corporation in 1624, and the Troutbecks, whose descendant the Earl of Shrewsbury sold his part in 1666. The old gateway was flanked by two towers. The high octagonal tower on the left was built in 1601 by John Tyrer, a lay clerk at the cathedral, to raise water from the Dee and pipe it into the city.

93

Neale T. Evans

The Watergate, 1993

Watercolour over pen & ink
26 × 36.6 cm
Commissioned 1993.91

The Watergate was rebuilt in 1788 to replace a medieval archway. Like the Eastgate, it is built of red sandstone with a rusticated arch, but with only one passage for pedestrians. As its name implies, the Watergate of the Middle Ages stood near the edge of the Dee, and was the main entrance to the city for goods which were unloaded from the wharves. The Dee gradually silted up, so in the 1730s a 'cut' was made, canalising the river. New wharves sprang up a little way downstream, and Crane Street was built to link them with the Watergate.

94

George Pickering (1794-1857)

The Shipgate

Pencil 15.3 × 23.8 cm
Presented by T. Cann Hughes 1925.1

In the early 19th century a road called Skinners Lane ran between the wall and the river, flanked by the workshops of animal skinners and an acid factory. In the early 1830s the county acquired this industrial area and extended the city wall to enclose it. As part of this work the Shipgate, a few yards south-west of the Bridgegate, was demolished in 1831. The Shipgate led to St Mary's Hill, the packhorse route from the town centre to the river. The archway of the Shipgate was later re-erected in Grosvenor Park.

95

96

97

96

UNKNOWN ARTIST
(LATE 19TH CENTURY)

The Bridgegate

Etching 12.5 × 17.8 cm
Presented by B.S. Lewis 1956.86(b)

The medieval Bridgegate was demolished in 1781, and the present gate was designed by Joseph Turner and built in 1782 at the Corporation's expense. It is of buff sandstone, with a rusticated segmental arch flanked by arched pedestrian passages and topped by balustrades. This view from Lower Bridge Street also shows the *Old Edgar* and the *Bear and Billet* to the right, with the great bulk of the Dee Mills beyond the Bridgegate.

97

WILLIAM ROBERT WRIGHT BOYD
(1877-1963)

The Newgate, 1939

Pen & ink with bodycolour over pencil
31.6 × 38.7 cm
Purchased 1982.31

The Wolfgate had become a bottleneck for traffic by the late 1920s, so it was decided to build a wider opening to the south of it. The Newgate was designed by Sir Walter and Michael Tapper. Built of reinforced concrete and faced with red Runcorn sandstone, it was opened in 1938. It has a single wide archway flanked by towers, and is a fine example of austere 1930s Gothic Revival architecture. Beyond the Newgate lie the remains of the largest stone-built Roman amphitheatre known in Britain, discovered in 1929 when the foundations were being dug for an extension to the Ursuline Convent School.

98

98

ARTHUR GODWIN (1900-89)

The Wolfgate

Etching 14.7 × 10.7 cm
Presented by the Estate of Miss Dandy 1968.88(e)

When the Newgate opened in 1938, Pepper Street and its continuation, Little St John Street, were diverted from the former Newgate or Wolfgate just to the north. In the Middle Ages this was a postern gate. It was rebuilt in 1608, and again in the late 1760s, making the Wolfgate the oldest remaining gateway in the city walls. The battlements above were added in 1890. Outside it can now be seen the foundation of the south-east angle tower of the Roman fortress.

99

99

'DRAWAZA'

Chester Castle from the North, 1772

Etching & engraving 12.3 × 16.4 cm
Presented 1965.235

Chester Castle is built on a knoll in the south-western corner of the area enclosed by the city walls. It is sited to overlook the strategic bridge across the river Dee leading to North Wales, as well as the former harbour area of the city. The castle was founded in 1070 by William the Conqueror when he brought his army to Chester to put down a revolt. William also founded the County Palatine of Chester in 1070, when he granted the county to his kinsman Hugh Lupus to hold from the Crown with full independent jurisdiction.

100

NATHANIEL BUCK (AFTER 1696-BEFORE 1779) AFTER SAMUEL BUCK (1696-1779)

The North-West View of Chester Castle, 1727

Engraving 19 × 36.8 cm
Purchased 1954.265(c)

Chester Castle became the seat of the earls of Chester and the centre of government for the County Palatine of Chester. The first castle was of motte and bailey type. The *motte* or earth mound still survives in the inner bailey, but the original timber towers and palisades were presumably soon rebuilt in stone. The 12th-century Agricola Tower probably incorporates the early gateway into the castle. The 12th-century Flag Tower surmounts the top of the motte and perhaps replaced a timber tower. The original castle may have consisted only of the inner bailey, with the outer bailey being a later addition.

101

AFTER JOHN BOYDELL (1719-1804)

View of Chester from the South-West, 1749

Engraving 20.4 × 32 cm
Presented 1965.258(b)

The earldom of Chester was united to the Crown in 1237, and since 1245 the title has been borne by the monarch's eldest son. After the 1290s no major changes occurred to Chester Castle for several centuries. The buildings were kept in good repair until the 16th century, but by the mid-17th century the gateways and other sections had become partly ruined. During the Jacobite rebellion of 1745 the castle was again put into a state of readiness. A gun battery was built to the south of the outer gateway, and another on the south-western curtain wall overlooking the river and bridge.

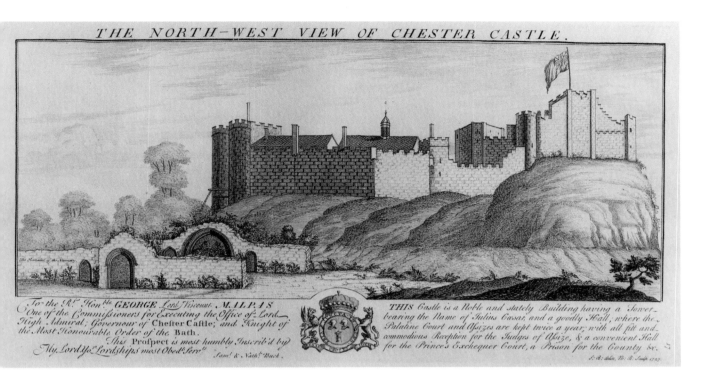

THE NORTH-WEST VIEW OF CHESTER CASTLE.

To the Rt. Honble. GEORGE Lord Viscount MALPAS One of the Commissioners for Executing the Office of Lord High Admiral; Governour of Chester Castle; and Knight of the Most Honourable Order of the Bath.
This Prospect is most humbly Inscrib'd by My Lord Yor. Lordships most Obedt. Servt. Saml. & Nathl. Buck.

THIS Castle is a Noble and stately Building having a Tower bearing the Name of Julius Caesar, and a goodly Hall, where the Palatine Court and Assizes are kept twice a year, with all fit and commodious Reception for the Judges of Assize, & a convenient Hall for the Prince's Exchequer Court, a Prison for the County &c.

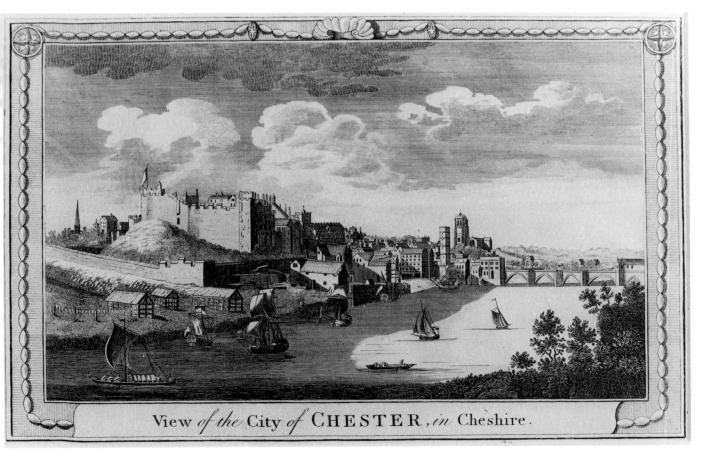

View of the City of CHESTER, in Cheshire.

WILLIAM BYRNE (1743-1805) AFTER
JOSEPH MALLORD WILLIAM TURNER
(1775-1851)

*The South-West Corner of
Chester Castle, 1810*

Engraving 22.5 × 28.2 cm
Presented by Sir Wyndham R. Dunstan
1942.291

This picture shows the medieval domestic quarters along the inner bailey's south-west wall. From the late 11th century the castle was of both strategic and administrative importance, since Chester was the base from which North Wales was conquered in the 12th and 13th centuries. The two most important institutions of the County Palatine of Chester, the Exchequer and County Court, were based at the castle, which also served as a garrison and prison. All these functions continued into the 19th century. Although it was geographically within Chester's city walls, the castle remained outside the city's jurisdiction until local government reorganisation in 1974.

102

103

MOSES GRIFFITH (1747-1819)

The Old Dee Bridge and Chester Castle

Pen & ink with watercolour
33.8 × 51.9 cm
Presented by Miss Margaret S. Davies
1962.98

Towards the left of the picture rises the Agricola Tower, which stands at the north-east corner of the inner bailey. It contains three chambers, the lowest one rebuilt after a fire in the early 14th century. The middle chamber is a chapel of the late 12th or early 13th century, named St Mary de Castro (St Mary's in the Castle), which has fragments of ornamental 14th-century wall paintings. To the right of the Agricola Tower is the long roof of the Shire Hall with its central cupola, and towards the centre of the picture is the church of St Mary-on-the-Hill.

103

104

104

MOSES GRIFFITH (1747-1819)

The Outer Gateway, Chester Castle, 1776

Pen & ink with watercolour
30.1 × 38.8 cm
Presented by Alderman E. Peter Jones
1939.330

The principal entrance to the outer bailey was built in 1292-3. Facing north, its two tall half-drum towers flanked a drawbridge across the moat, which was cut to the bedrock more than eight metres below the present-day surface. The gateway's site is now the car park in front of 'A' block. By long-established tradition, criminals sentenced to death in the County Court were handed over for execution to the city sheriffs at Gloverstone, a kind of no-man's land outside this gateway.

105

MOSES GRIFFITH (1747-1819)

The Outer Bailey, Chester Castle

Pen & ink with watercolour
30.1 × 46.2 cm
Presented by Alderman E. Peter Jones
1939.329

Following the Crown's annexation of the earldom of Chester in 1237, considerable work was done at Chester Castle by Henry III and Edward I, particularly in the outer bailey, where the palisade was replaced by a stone wall in 1247-51. Along the south-eastern side of the outer bailey were the chief administrative buildings, the Shire Hall and the Exchequer. Another moat divided the outer from the inner bailey, and a bridge across it led to a gateway facing north-east. The well-house, on the right of this picture, was in the middle of the outer bailey.

105

106

MOSES GRIFFITH (1747-1819)

Old County Hall, Chester Castle

Pen & ink with watercolour
26.3 × 36.3 cm
Presented by Alderman E. Peter Jones
1939.328

The old County Hall was also known
as the Great Hall or Shire Hall.
Originally built in 1250-3 and rebuilt in
1579-81, it housed the courts of the
justices of the county. At its south end
was the Exchequer Court of the
County Palatine of Chester, and it was
in this hall that the citizens of Chester
completed the capitulation of the city
to Parliament on 3 February 1646. By
the end of the 18th century much of
the medieval castle was ruinous, so an
Act of Parliament was obtained for
rebuilding the outer bailey, and after a
competition Thomas Harrison was
commissioned as architect.

107

107

THOMAS HARRISON (1744-1829)

*View from the Portico of Chester
Castle*

Pen & ink with sepia wash
31.5 × 51.8 cm
Purchased 1952.95

In 1788 Thomas Harrison began the
reconstruction of the outer bailey to
form the present Neo-Classical
monument. From 1789 the Great Hall

and other buildings on the south-
eastern side were replaced by the
central block. 'B' block, on the viewer's
left, was completed in 1807, replacing
part of the inner bailey curtain wall
and gateway. Part of the outer bailey
curtain wall and gateway was demolished in 1809-10 and 'A' block, on the
viewer's right, was built over part of
the infilled moat. The final element in
this new scheme was the grand
entrance or Propylaeum of 1811-5.

108

GEORGE CUITT (1779-1854)

Chester Castle from Nun's Gardens, 1827

Etching 31.8 × 25.4 cm
Presented by E. Gardner Williams
1960.148(115)

The grand entrance or Propylaeum is a massive gateway in the Greek Doric order flanked by two smaller pedimented lodges. It is a free-standing monumental structure like the Brandenburg Gate of 1789-93 in Berlin, and Harrison's contemporaries recognised its similarity to the Propylaeum of the Acropolis in Athens. The Gothic arch in the picture is the remains of the Benedictine nunnery of St Mary. The site, known as Nun's Gardens, was purchased by the county in 1806, and the arch was later re-erected in Grosvenor Park.

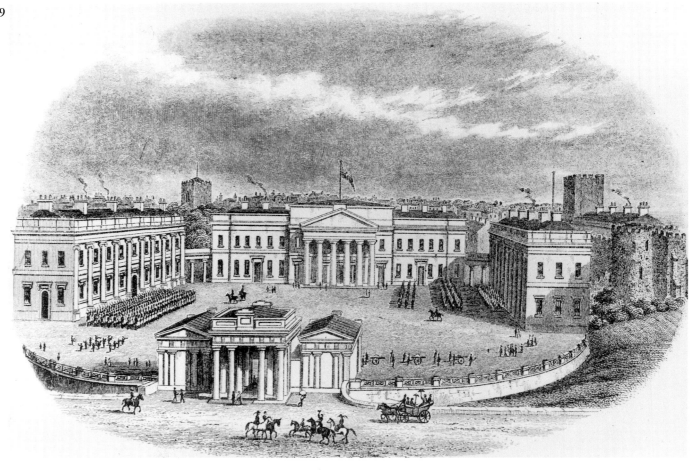

109

EVANS & GRESTY (ACTIVE 1854-60)

Chester Castle, Barracks and Assize Courts

Engraving 8.5 × 11.2 cm
Presented by Mrs. Bradbury 1973.32(f)

Thomas Harrison's Chester Castle is 'one of the most powerful monuments of the Greek Revival in the whole of England' (Nikolaus Pevsner). The middle part of the central block projects slightly and is ashlared, whilst the side pieces are rusticated. Six giant unfluted Doric columns carry a pediment below the heavy attic, behind which is the semicircular Shire Hall. Small Doric colonnades link the centre to the side blocks, which have an order of giant unfluted Ionic half-columns. 'B' block on the right housed the armoury, while 'A' block contained barracks and the Exchequer Court, one of the institutions of the Palatinate which was abolished in 1830.

110

JOHN GRESTY (ACTIVE 1850-82)

Chester Castle and Savings Bank

Lithograph 20.8 × 28.7 cm
Presented by T.A.Gresty 1956.18(d)

The main ranges of Thomas Harrison's castle form three sides of a large semicircular parade ground or esplanade, which is on the site of the former outer bailey but is much bigger. Harrison took care to maintain the scenic relationship between his Neo-Classical buildings and the remaining medieval ones, and in 1818 he refaced the Agricola Tower, the main medieval survival, with red sandstone. The Savings Bank (now a restaurant) on the left of this picture was built in the Tudor Gothic style by James Harrison in 1851-3.

111

WILLIAM TASKER (1808-52)

The High Sheriff's Procession Passing Chester Castle, 1845

Pencil, pen & ink, grey wash & white bodycolour 20 × 33 cm
Purchased with grant-aid from the V&A Purchase Grant Fund and the National Art Collections Fund 1980.74

This picture, dated 29 March 1845, shows the procession of Sir W.M. Stanley, High Sheriff of Cheshire, passing Chester Castle on his way to meet the Judge of Assize. Chester was an important centre of legal administration. Visits of judges were attended with elaborate ceremonial, and the gentry of the county arrived in the city in large numbers. The opening of the twice-yearly Great Sessions or Assizes was normally marked by a sermon preached at the cathedral.

112

FRANCIS NICHOLSON (1753-1844)

Chester Castle and Skinner's Yard

Watercolour over pencil 43 × 62.1 cm
Presented by H.K. Frost 1936.89

In the early 19th century a road called Skinner's Lane ran between the city walls and the river Dee. It housed the workshops of animal skinners and an acid factory, plus several warehouses and small mills. The boats which serviced these premises were known as Mersey flats. This picture shows the stark contrast between the cream-coloured Manley stone of Thomas Harrison's principal buildings and the dark red sandstone of the rest of the castle.

112

113

WILLIAM TASKER (1808-52)

Chester Castle and the River Dee

Pencil with white bodycolour and pen & ink 20.1 × 34.3 cm
Purchased 1987.51

In 1830 the county purchased the industrial area between the castle and the river. The buildings were demolished, and a very high wall of massive masonry was built to enclose the site, around which the promenade of the city walls was extended. The justices' apartments and officers' barracks on the south-east side of the upper bailey were also demolished in 1830. The new block along the south-west side—prominent in this drawing—was built to house an armoury on the ground floor and barracks on the two upper storeys.

114

HENRY PETHER (1828-65)

Chester Castle by Moonlight

Oil on canvas 59.6 × 90 cm
Presented by the National Art Collections Fund 1959.7

At the far left of this painting is the Trustee Savings Bank of 1851-3 with its corner turret. The focus of the picture is Chester Castle, showing the gaol on the river side. Immediately to the right of the Castle is the low tower of St Mary-on-the-Hill, which was raised in 1861-2. Further to the right can be seen the tower of St John the Baptist (which collapsed in 1881), and the Dee Mills (demolished in 1910), then the Old Dee Bridge and the fishermen's cottages of Handbridge. The painting shows salmon fishing in progress on the River Dee.

115

GEORGE CUITT (1779-1854)

Chester from the South-East

Etching 10.8 × 17 cm
Presented by A.O. Orrett 1963.54(c)

An important element in Thomas
Harrison's rebuilding of Chester Castle
was the gaol behind the central block.
The architect James Elmes, writing in
1817, said: 'no-one viewing this edifice
can possibly mistake it for anything but
a gaol, the openings as small as
convenient and the whole external
appearance made as gloomy and
melancholy as possible.' This picture
shows how the riverside elevation
towered dramatically over its original
setting of small dwellings and
warehouses.

116

THOMAS ALLOM (1804-72)

*The Old Dee Bridge and Chester
Castle*

Sepia wash over pencil 9.7 × 15.5 cm
Purchased 1957.111

This drawing clearly depicts Thomas
Harrison's gaol, which was laid out on
a half-octagonal plan behind the
central block. The gaoler's house was
built on the same level as the entrance
and court-room. To its south-east the
ground falls steeply, and the windows
of the house overlooked the five
courtyards in which prisoners were
housed and exercised. This arrange-
ment accorded with the 'panoptic'
principle, giving the gaoler full
supervision of his charges. The prison
chapel was beneath his house.

117

LOUISE RAYNER (1832-1924)

Chester Castle from the River Dee

Watercolour with bodycolour
24.9 × 42.5 cm
Presented by Alderman E. Peter Jones
1965.184

The gaol at Chester Castle was taken
over by the Government in 1877 and
closed in 1884. Eventually the cell
blocks were demolished, and in 1900-2
the site was made into a drill ground
for the local artillery. The high wall of
massive masonry which surrounded
the old gaol and extended to the city
walls was taken down, and the City
Corporation created Castle Drive,
running from Grosvenor Road to the
Bridgegate. To the right of this picture
is the church of St Mary-on-the-Hill,
the upper part of whose tower dates
from a restoration of 1861-2 by James
Harrison.

118

BERNARD L. HOWARD

County Hall, Chester, 1994

Watercolour over pencil 51.7 × 73.1 cm
Commissioned 1994.15

The castle's central block had been
used as the administrative headquarters
of Cheshire County Council since its
formation in 1888, but the growing
complexity of the county council's
functions made more space necessary.
The large Neo-Georgian block of
County Hall was designed by the
County Architect, E. Mainwaring
Parkes, and built in 1938-57. It
occupies the site of Harrison's gaol
and is attached to the former gaoler's
house. The increasing number of staff
rapidly outgrew County Hall, and
other offices in Chester are now used
as well.

119

119

THOMAS SHOTTER BOYS (1803-74)
AFTER GEORGE CUITT (1779-1854)

Lamb Row, 1833

Watercolour with bodycolour
15.7 × 23 cm
Presented by Alderman E. Peter Jones
1952.9

Chester's world-famous Rows are a
unique system of continuous, covered
walkways built into the fronts of the
buildings at first-floor level. With
shops on both levels, the Rows provide
Chester's most distinctive architectural
feature. The origin of the Rows is still
unclear, but it is significant that the
extent of the Rows largely coincides
with the area once covered by the
Roman fortress, the ruins of whose
massive stone buildings survived into
the Middle Ages. In medieval Chester,
narrow property strips were set at right
angles to the main streets. In them
were constructed typical merchants'
houses consisting of a hall and shops,
built of stone or timber, over a secure
stone cellar. At Chester the shallow
bedrock kept the cellar floors almost
level with the street, which lifted the
hall and shops—and the walkway in
front of them—up to first-floor level.
Although these early Rows were
reached by steps, the banked Roman
rubble behind the streets meant that
the back doors were at ground level
again.

120

George Cuitt (1779-1854)

Eastgate Row North

Etching 5.3 × 7.2 cm
Presented by E. Gardner Williams
1960.148(10)

The Rows probably started to develop towards the end of the 13th century. Chester was the base for King Edward I's Welsh campaigns, and the wealth created by supplying the army prompted a building boom. As the street frontages filled up, so the elevated galleries in front of individual buildings could be linked together to form almost continuous walkways. This process may have been consolidated by widespread rebuilding after a catastrophic fire in 1278. From the early 16th century the chambers above the Rows were often enlarged and had to be supported by posts set in the street, and small shops were later built between the posts at street level. By the 17th century some of the Rows were being enclosed. New brick

120

façades were added by the Georgians, while the Victorians restored or copied many of the old buildings. The Rows were first legally protected by the City Council in 1845, and the narrow plots, divided ownership and mutual need for access have helped to ensure the survival of the Rows to this day.

121

George Thompson

The Cross, 1993

Watercolour over pencil 35.4 × 56.2 cm
Commissioned 1993.108

The Rows occur along the four main streets which radiate from the Cross at the heart of the City. The medieval Cross was taken down in 1646 but was rebuilt here in 1975. The corner of Bridge Street and Watergate Street was rebuilt in 1892 for the 1st Duke of Westminster by Thomas Meakin Lockwood, who had earlier designed the opposite corner of Bridge Street and Eastgate Street. Lockwood's high building combines many materials— half-timbering, red brick patterned with blue, plus stone bands and dressings—together with Tudor, Renaissance and 'Queen Anne' details.

121

122

LOUISE RAYNER (1832-1924)

*God's Providence House,
Watergate Street*

Watercolour with bodycolour
26.8 × 12.5 cm
Presented by Miss B. Cann Hughes
1950.717

Flanked by Georgian brick buildings
and dated 1652, this is one of Chester's
most famous timber-framed houses.
The inscription, 'God's Providence is
Mine Inheritance', is said to refer to
the house's escape from an outbreak
of the plague. This picture shows the
house before 1861, when the owner
proposed to demolish it. The Chester
Archaeological Society, which was
encouraging the half-timber revival,
protested strongly, and some of the
original timbers were used when it was
rebuilt in a larger and more ornate
form by James Harrison in 1862.

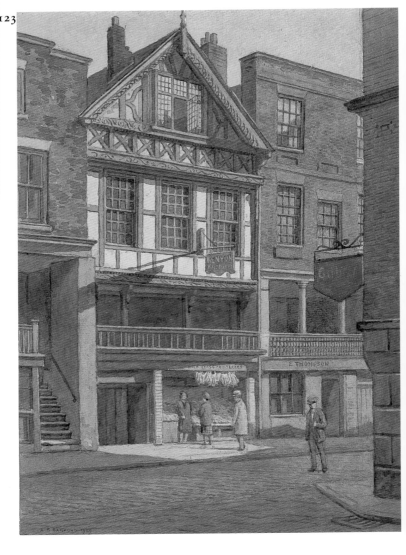

123

ALFRED BENNETT BAMFORD
(1857-1939)

*Leche House, Watergate Street,
1929*

Watercolour over pencil 32.6 × 23.3 cm
Presented by Chester College of Further
Education 1965.71

This small half-timbered building is
one of the best-preserved town houses
in the Rows. Inside is an undercroft,
which probably dates from the 14th
century. Above is a late 15th-century
great hall set back at right angles to the
street, complete with its original gallery
and private rooms, and still open to the
roof. The façade with carved timbers
and posts is early 17th century and still
has its Georgian sash windows. The
house became the property of
Alderman John Leche (d.1639), who
was a descendant of the surgeon or
'leech' to King Edward III.

124

LOUISE RAYNER (1832-1924)

South Side of Watergate Street

Watercolour with bodycolour
46.7 × 59.6 cm
Presented by Mrs A. Mabel Irwin
1975.253

This picture shows the south side of
Watergate Street looking east. On the
right is Bishop Lloyd's Palace, one of
Britain's most decorative timber-
framed buildings. It is named after
George Lloyd, Bishop of Sodor and
Man (1599-1605) and of Chester
(1605-15), and is dated 1615, the year
of his death. The richly carved panels
on the façade include the three Legs of
Man and scenes from the Bible. The
two rooms above the Row have
decorative stucco chimneypieces and
ceilings. This picture shows the house
before Thomas Meakin Lockwood's
restoration of 1899-1900, when he
replaced the Georgian sash windows
with leaded lights.

125

THOMAS BAILEY (ACTIVE 1828-64)

South Side of Watergate Street, 1837

Pencil 21.8 × 30.6 cm
Presented by Alderman E. Peter Jones
1943.330(35)

The south side of Watergate Street is
seen here looking west, with Bishop
Lloyd's Palace on the left. In Tudor
times this was known as
Fleshmongers' Row, because the
butchers' stalls were situated here.
Watergate Street led to the medieval
port, but became less fashionable as
the port declined and thus escaped the
large-scale Victorian rebuilding which
transformed the appearance of
Chester's other main streets. Part of
this Row became derelict in the 20th
century and was rebuilt in 1968-70:
although modern in material (shut-
tered concrete) and style, it retains the
scale and character of the Row.

126

THOMAS SHOTTER BOYS (1803-74)

Watergate Row South, 1862

Watercolour 21.2 × 29.4 cm
Purchased with grant-aid from the
National Art Collections Fund 1961.44

This view, looking west, shows the
Row at Bishop Lloyd's Palace. The
brackets on the wooden posts have
fine 17th-century carvings. Facing the
street there are fearsome bearded
giants holding up the building, while in
the Row are some charming baby
animals. Each section of Row has a
raised and sloping stallboard on the
street side. As seen here, they were
(and still are) used as stalls for the
display of goods and as places where
people could stand and watch the
street scene below.

127

JOHN ROMNEY (1786-1863)

Mainwaring House, Watergate Street, 1822

Engraving 12.8 × 16.2 cm
1965.263

This timber-framed house on the north side of Watergate Street belonged to the Mainwaring family. George Mainwaring (d.1695) established the family's connection with

Chester. He was born in London but married into a Chester family, becoming mayor in 1681-2 and one of the city's M.P.s in 1689. In 1852 Mainwaring House was replaced by a brick terrace of five large Victorian houses, set back from the street. Although they do not contain a Row, their front doors are still at first-floor level. The house to the left was built in the early 18th century by Alderman Henry Bennett.

128

RICHARD HORE

Booth Mansion, Watergate Street, 1994

Pencil 59.4 × 42 cm
Commissioned 1994.12

Booth Mansion is the largest house in Watergate Street. In 1700 Alderman George Booth converted two 13th-century dwellings into a new house. The Row frontage is supported on Tuscan columns, but the Row itself is spanned by medieval arches. It is said that the handsome brick façade was deliberately built forward at an angle so that it could be admired from the Cross. Alderman Booth died in 1719 and soon afterwards his splendid house became an Assembly Room, the scene of many fashionable balls and entertainments during the 18th century.

129

LOUISE RAYNER (1832-1924)

Watergate Row North

Watercolour with bodycolour
21.8 × 31.9 cm
Purchased with grant-aid from the V&A Purchase Grant Fund, the National Art Collections Fund and Sotheby's Chester 1978.109

This view down the Row from the Cross shows the sign for 'Muras Late Youde/Furniture Broker'. Eliza Muras, Furniture Dealer at 4 Watergate Row North is recorded in 1892-6, and some of her goods are displayed on the stallboard. A hanging lamp advertises the *Deva Hotel*, which conceals 16th- and 17th-century woodwork behind a

Georgian façade. Some of the buildings further down this Row were rebuilt in the late 1970s and '80s in a variety of styles, but they all carefully preserve the line of the medieval Row. Across the street, to the left, may be seen the rebuilt façade of God's Providence House.

130

WILLIAM CALLOW (1812–1908)

Shoemakers' Row, Northgate Street, 1854

Watercolour with bodycolour over pencil 40.3 × 63.2 cm
Purchased with grant-aid from the National Art Collections Fund
1954.292

Northgate Street was the main route to the market place and, unlike Chester's other three principal streets, its southern end was medieval and not Roman in origin. There were only two short sections of Row along Northgate Street. Shoemakers' Row was on the west side. 19th-century pictures like this show the original Shoemakers' Row to have been a ramshackle range of crumbling timber buildings. It had four inns or taverns, all of which have now disappeared except the *Dublin Packet*, which once fronted Northgate Street but now has its main entrance in the Market Square.

131

MICHAEL GORDON-LEE

Shoemakers' Row, Northgate Street, 1994

Pastel 37.7 × 55 cm
Commissioned 1994.13

Shoemakers' Row was rebuilt between 1897 and 1909 as part of a City Council road widening project. It was the most far-reaching development scheme to affect the Rows in the 19th century, since it involved replacing a true Row with a ground-level covered walkway. John Douglas had first proposed this scheme in 1886, and he was one of the architects responsible for this ambitious and very picturesque group of black-and-white buildings. Douglas designed nos.5-13, on the left of this picture, in 1900, and his pupil James Strong designed the even more elaborate building beside it in 1909.

132

ALFRED BENNETT BAMFORD
(1857-1939)

Blue Bell Inn, Northgate Street, 1930

Watercolour over pencil 23.9 × 32.9 cm
Presented by Chester College of Further Education 1965.175

The former *Blue Bell Inn* is part of a small group of buildings known as Lorimers' Row. The upper floors are built over the pavement to form an arcade. This is a feature common to the main streets of Chester beyond the Rows, and is preserved when re-building takes place. The *Blue Bell* is a fairly intact pair of medieval buildings, extended and made into a single property in the 18th century. A unique survival is the detached shopfront between the pavement and the road.

132

133

133

GEORGE BATENHAM
(ACTIVE FROM 1794, d.1833)

East Side of Northgate Street

Etching 24.9 × 38.5 cm
Presented by Miss Estelle Dyke 1963.36(4)

This short stretch of Row still preserves something of its former character. Always a rather dark and neglected area, it was once known as Broken Shin Row because the paving was so uneven! Three of the 17th-century buildings at the southern end of the Row survived into the early 19th century, although much of their timber-framing had been plastered over and most of the casements had been replaced by sash windows. By the steps to Eastgate Row North is seen a lamplighter trimming an oil lamp, the only means of illuminating Chester's streets before the introduction of gas.

134

LOUISE RAYNER (1832-1924)

Eastgate Row North

Watercolour with bodycolour
27.8 × 13.8 cm
Presented by F.T. Haswell 1949.433

Unlike the other Rows, the western end of Eastgate Row North disappeared behind buildings fronting the street and sloped down almost to the level of Northgate Street. For this reason it was known as the Dark Row or Dark Lofts from at least the 15th century, although by the 19th century it was called Pepper Alley Row. Always the gloomiest and most isolated stretch of the Rows, it had a reputation for attracting rowdy and immoral behaviour. As this picture shows, the Rows were not particularly salubrious places in the 18th and 19th centuries.

135

LOUISE RAYNER (1832-1924)

North Side of Eastgate Street

Watercolour with bodycolour
22 × 28.1 cm
Presented by Miss B. Cann Hughes
1950.721

In medieval times the Row buildings at the north-west corner of Eastgate Street were known as the Buttershops, where butter, milk and other dairy products were sold. All the buildings in front of the Dark Row were rebuilt after this view was painted. Nos. 5-7 in the centre were rebuilt in the vernacular revival style by Thomas Meakin Lockwood in 1874, and the semi-circular black-and-white façade on the corner dates from 1898. Nos. 11-13 were rebuilt by Lockwood for Richard Jones's department store in 1898-9, and were extended to either side in the 1920s.

136

JULIA MIDGLEY

*Eastgate Row Development
under Construction, 1993*

Watercolour & bodycolour with pen &
ink 35.7 × 55.1 cm
Commissioned 1993.109

Nos. 3-15 Eastgate Street and 2-8
Northgate Street were largely
occupied from the mid-1960s until
1990 by the Owen Owen department
store. The owner of the site, Refuge
Assurance plc, undertook a major
development in 1991-3. Designed by
Simon Johnson of Biggins Sargent
Partnership, the imaginative scheme
has brought new life to a long-
neglected part of the Rows. The
buildings in Northgate Street and nos.
5-7 Eastgate Street (now occupied by
Beaverbrooks) have been refurbished.
The Dark Row has been raised and,
most importantly, opened up to the
street, with the traditional stallboard
and balustrade plus small enclosed
shops.

136

137

JOHN GRESTY (ACTIVE 1850-82)

Eastgate Street and the Eastgate

Lithograph 21 × 28.9 cm
Presented by T.A. Gresty 1956.18(e)

Always the most prosperous of
Chester's shopping streets, Eastgate
Street was extensively rebuilt in the
second half of the 19th century. On
the right of this picture is Bolland's,
'Confectioners by Royal Appointment
and Suppliers of Queen Victoria's
Wedding Cake'. Bolland's and the
building beside it were designed by
Thomas Mainwaring Penson in 1855,
and are the earliest of Chester's black-
and-white revival buildings to survive.
Eastgate Row South ends at what is
now the entrance to the Grosvenor
Precinct. Beyond may be seen the
colonnaded arcade of the *Royal Hotel*,
replaced in 1863-6 by Chester's famous
Grosvenor Hotel, also designed by
Penson.

137

138

UNKNOWN ARTIST
(EARLY 19TH CENTURY)

South Side of Eastgate Street

Watercolour with pen & ink
20.8 × 22.5 cm
Presented by Alderman E. Peter Jones
1952.10

The Row on the south side of Eastgate
Street is easily the busiest today. The
Row walkway in this picture, thought to
date from *c.*1817-28, disappears behind
the enclosed chambers which replace
the usual stallboard. The erection of
small shops in the Rows, common in
the 17th century, was frequently
criticised because they blocked out
both light and air to the Rows. Most
were removed in the 18th and 19th
centuries and only one enclosed stretch
of Row, on the south side of Eastgate
Street, now survives.

138

139

139

LOUISE RAYNER (1832-1924)

Bridge Street Row East

Watercolour with bodycolour
12.7 × 17.7 cm
Purchased 1970.26

This view is taken inside Bridge Street
Row East at the Cross, and shows how
low and dark the Row was before its
rebuilding in 1888. The darkness of
the Row contrasts with the sunshine
outside, where tram lines and the south
wall of St Peter's can be seen. Just
visible on the left is the window of a
tiny shop occupying the width of the
stallboard. The shop on the right was
run by John Wild, hosier and glover,
between at least 1878 and 1896, and
thus continued in occupation after the
rebuilding.

140

140

BERTHA GORST (BORN 1873,
ACTIVE 1897-1929)

*Corner of Bridge Street and
Eastgate Street, 1909*

Etching 17.2 × 25 cm
Purchased 1993.2

The black-and-white buildings at the
Cross, with their ornate corner turret,
are undoubtedly the most photographed in Chester. Designed by
Thomas Meakin Lockwood in 1888 for
the 1st Duke of Westminster, this
picturesque corner group is typical of
the Victorian fashion for building in
the style of the timber-framed houses
of the Tudor period. Like so many of
Chester's late 19th-century buildings,
the detail and craftsmanship are
outstanding.

141

THOMAS BAILEY (ACTIVE 1828-64)

East Side of Bridge Street, 1837

Pencil 22 × 30.4 cm
1965.213

This drawing shows the great width of the street. Bridge Street Row East has always been busy and prosperous. It was originally known as Mercers' Row because the cloth dealers had their stalls here. Some of the late 18th-century brick houses in Bridge Street still survive. Most of the city's streets looked like this before so much of Chester was rebuilt in the black-and-white style in the second half of the 19th century. The street is lit by gas lamps: Chester's first gas works had been established in 1817, and by 1831 gas had reached all parts of the city.

142

RICHARD HORE

St Michael's Row, 1994

Pencil 41.9 × 59.3 cm
Commissioned 1994.11

St Michael's Buildings were designed by W.T. Lockwood in 1910 for the 2nd Duke of Westminster. The spacious arcade inside is a remarkably early example of an elevated shopping street. It now leads to the Grosvenor Precinct, which was built in 1963-5 and fits behind the main streets without disturbing the historic frontages. St Michael's Row is faced with Renaissance style white faience. The Bridge Street façade was originally faced in the same material, which many thought unsuited to the historic character of the Rows. The Duke gave way to public opinion, and the massive building was reclad with half-timbering in 1911.

143

GEORGE CUITT (1779-1854)

Bridge Street Row East, 1809

Etching 24.5 × 20.9 cm
Presented by E. Gardner Williams
1960.148(27c)

The southern end of Bridge Street Row East is spanned by the tower of St Michael's Church. To the left can be seen the 'Three Old Arches', dating from c.1200. The three round-headed stone arches are thought to be the earliest surviving shop front in Britain, and behind them are parts of a substantial 14th-century stone town house. The three arches are too thin to support heavy masonry, and the upper storeys were probably half-timbered in the Middle Ages. The arches are now incorporated into an 18th-century frontage. This section of Row is unique because there is no stallboard.

141

142

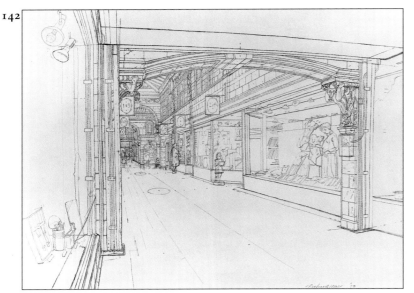

143

144

THOMAS BAILEY (ACTIVE 1828-64)

Lower Bridge Street, looking North, 1837

Pencil 22.1 × 30 cm
1965.214

There were originally Rows along both sides of Lower Bridge Street, forming the only example of Rows outside the site of the Roman fortress. They were gradually lost through enclosure and rebuilding during the late 17th and 18th centuries, but the remains of the enclosed western Row are clearly visible on the left of this picture. The large structure further up the street is Bridge House, built in the early 18th century for John Williams, Attorney-General of Cheshire, and now the Oddfellows Hall. Double steps originally swept up to a first-floor door, but the ground level is now obscured by shops.

144

Lower Bridge St.

145

MARJORIE CHRISTINE BATES
(1883-1962)

Falcon Inn, Lower Bridge Street

Colour lithograph 12.9 × 17.7 cm
Bequeathed by Councillor S.H.M.
Lloyd 1989.107

The *Falcon* was once the town house of the Grosvenor family. Built above a 13th-century cellar, it is said to date from 1626, and the Row running through the front of the building was enclosed in 1643. The sandstone Row piers, which supported the upper floor, can be seen inside the building. The *Falcon* was an inn between 1778 and 1878, before being altered by John Douglas as a temperance cocoa house for the 1st Duke of Westminster. Its present appearance owes much to a restoration of *c.*1886 by Grayson & Ould, and it was restored again as a public house in 1979-82.

145

Marjorie C. Bates.

146

GEORGE CUITT (1779-1854)

Interior of Lamb Row, 1819

Etching 13.9 × 20.2 cm
Presented by E. Gardner Williams
1960.148(112)

Lamb Row was built in 1655 for
Randle Holme III, an armorial painter
and antiquary who published an
heraldic encyclopaedia, *The Academy of
Armoury*, in 1688. The timber-framed
house, which projected well into the
street, was later converted into the
Lamb Inn. By the early 19th century the
dilapidated structure was considered to
be the most picturesque building in
Chester and was depicted by many
artists before its sudden collapse in
1821.

147

THOMAS BAILEY (ACTIVE 1828-64)

Undercroft in Bridge Street, 1840

Pencil 20.6 × 29.2 cm
Presented by Alderman E. Peter Jones
1943.330(51)

The undercroft was a typical feature of
medieval English houses, used to store
and display goods for sale. The vaulted
stone undercrofts in Chester are
unusual in being only a few feet below
ground. They were probably built for
very wealthy merchants, who wanted
their wares to be seen in the most
impressive surroundings. One of the
best, discovered in 1839, is at no.12
Bridge Street. Thought to date from
c.1270, it is 42 feet long and 15 feet
wide. Above it is the mid-17th-century
timber-framed home of the Cowper
family, two of whose members became
mayors of Chester.

148

LOUISE RAYNER (1832-1924)

West Side of Bridge Street

Watercolour with bodycolour
54.5 × 40.9 cm
Purchased with grant-aid from the
V&A Purchase Grant Fund 1966.31

This part of Bridge Street Row West
was formerly known as Scotch Row,
because tradesmen from Scotland
frequented it during the two great fairs
held each year in Chester. Half-way
along Bridge Street are the Dutch
Houses, a range of tall mid-17th-
century buildings. They are timber-
framed but plastered over, with
projecting floors and twisted columns.
Next door is an even taller building,
The Plane Tree, built by Thomas
Meakin Lockwood *c*.1873. It is half-
timbered and symmetrical, with an
elaborate projecting window and
balcony and flower patterns in the
plasterwork.

149

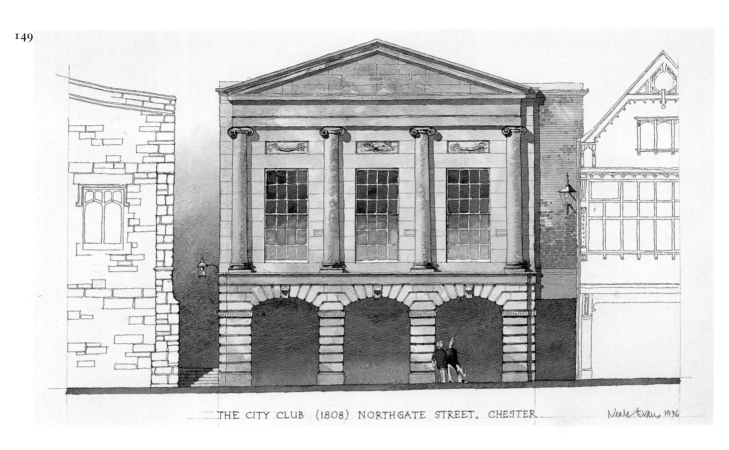

THE CITY CLUB (1808) NORTHGATE STREET, CHESTER Neale Evans 1996

149

NEALE T. EVANS

The City Club, Northgate Street,
1996

Watercolour with pen & ink over pencil
37.1 × 55.5 cm
Commissioned 1996.99

The City Club was designed by Thomas
Harrison and erected in 1807-8. The
ground floor was built as shops with
three glazed arches: it was refaced with
rusticated masonry *c.*1923, when a
passage was opened behind new
segmental arches to continue the
walkway of Shoemakers' Row. The
double-height news room above is
faced in smooth ashlar, with mono-
lithic Ionic half-columns carrying a
pediment and tall windows sur-
mounted by decorative panels. Now
the City Club, it was originally built as
the Commercial Coffee Room and
News Room, managed by a committee
representing one hundred
'proprietors'.

150

DAVID HODGSON (1798-1864)

The Exchange, Northgate Street,
1831

Oil on canvas 58.3 × 74.3 cm
Purchased with grant-aid from the
MGC/V&A Purchase Grant Fund
1989.146

The Exchange was built in 1695-8 in
the Market Square. Constructed of
brick with stone quoins, its upper
floors were originally carried over
colonnades, but part of the ground
floor was filled in for use as shops in
1756. The Exchange was used by the
Corporation for its meetings and
courts, and there was also an assembly
room for social events. The Exchange
was demolished after a fire on 30
December 1862. The single-storey
buildings to the south were the Green
Market (for vegetables) and the Fish
Market, with the Meat Market (or
Shambles) to the north.

151

LOUISE RAYNER (1832-1924)

The Town Hall, Northgate Street

Watercolour with bodycolour over
pencil 62.8 × 47.3 cm
Purchased 1952.149

The Exchange was replaced by the
Town Hall, designed by William Henry
Lynn of Belfast in the Gothic style of
the late 13th century and built in 1865-
9. With its tiers of Gothic windows,
prominent corner turrets and massive
central tower, the Town Hall's
inspiration was the Cloth Hall at Ypres,
the most impressive commercial
building of medieval northern Europe.
However, Lynn brought High
Victorian characteristics to his
interpretation by breaking the line of
the steeply pitched roof with dormer
windows, setting the spire diagonally
on the tower, and employing two
colours (buff and pink) for the
sandstone facing.

151

152

ALISTER WINTER ROBERTS

The Forum, Northgate Street, 1993

Watercolour over pencil 37.7 × 52.1 cm
Commissioned 1993.201

The Forum, a shopping precinct with City Council offices above, was opened in 1973. Its Modern architecture of concrete, brick and glass was designed by Michael Lyell Associates. The Forum replaced the old Market Hall with its Baroque façade of 1863 and the Gothic extension of 1880 which joined it to the Town Hall. These were both demolished in 1967, leaving only a fragment at the southern end. In 1993-5 the projecting offices were cut back, and the shopping precinct was remodelled by Leslie Jones with a Post-Modern façade of reconstituted stone and glass.

153

GEORGE BATENHAM (ACTIVE FROM 1794, d.1833)

West Side of Northgate Street, 1817

Etching 25 × 38.3 cm
Presented by E. Gardner Williams
1960.148(49)

To the left of this picture are the open wooden stalls of the Meat Market, which were soon replaced by a brick and stone structure. The large Georgian house behind them was the city residence of the Masseys of Moston near Chester: the site is now occupied by the *Shropshire Arms* public house. The half-timbered house to the right, demolished shortly after this print was made, was on the site of the Odeon Cinema. It last tenant was the artist James Hunter, who gave his name to the adjoining passage, Hunter's Walk, which became Hunter Street in the 1890s.

152

154

FRANCES SEBA SMITH

Chester Library, Northgate Street, 1995

Linoprint 43.2 × 67.6 cm
Commissioned 1995.533

The façade of elaborately-moulded terracotta and red brick was designed by Philip H. Lockwood and built in 1913-4 for the Westminster Coach and Motor Car Works. The site was already occupied by a coachworks and showroom, and it later became a motor-car showroom. From 1973-9 the building was run by the Chester Arts and Recreation Trust. The new Chester Library was designed by David Luxton of Cheshire County Architects and built in 1981-4, with a new four-storey structure behind the restored façade. This replaced a building in St John Street, which had opened as the Free Library in 1874.

154

155

BERNARD L. HOWARD

The Odeon Cinema, Northgate Street, 1995

Watercolour over pencil 35 × 55.6 cm
Commissioned 1995.196

The Odeon Cinema, opened in 1936, is one of the numerous provincial Odeons designed by Harry Weedon. Its Art Deco style, almost synonymous with the word 'Odeon', was frequently employed for 1930s cinemas. Chester's Odeon is an asymmetrical composition of rectangular blocks with a tower at the north end of Market Square. Both brickwork and windows are used in boldly-modelled bands, accentuating the height of the central section and giving a streamlined effect to the frontages on either side. Many Odeons were faced with ceramic blocks but, although the style was new, the traditional material of brick was used in Chester.

155

156

TOM MORTON

The Former Fire Station, Northgate Street, 1995

Watercolour over pencil 38.3 × 54 cm
Commissioned 1995.522

From 1863 Chester had a body of voluntary firemen, the Earl of Chester's Volunteer Fire Brigade. The Corporation provided a paid superintendent and the necessary firefighting equipment, and in 1914 assumed control of the brigade. The fire station in Northgate Street was built in 1911 to the design of James Strong, a pupil of John Douglas. The half-timbered building is richly decorated, with three semicircular oriel windows beneath overhanging gables. Built for three horse-drawn appliances, the fire station had become obsolete by the 1960s and a new one was opened in St Anne Street in 1970.

156

Chester : The Old Firestation

Tom Morton 1995

157

SUE HENDERSON

King's Buildings, King Street, 1995

Colour etching & aquatint
45.2 × 37.4 cm
Commissioned 1995.529

King Street was known as Barn Lane in the 13th century, since it led to a barn owned by St Werburgh's Abbey. With its gently sloping curve, King Street today is one of Chester's most pleasant side-streets. Most of its houses, dating from the 18th and 19th centuries, are individually undistinguished, but the effect of the street as a whole is attractive. At its west end stands a terrace of houses built in 1776 and known as King's Buildings. Since 1966 the inner ring road has run past the bay window at the end.

157

WILLIAM MONK (1863-1937)

Excavation in Deanery Field, 1935

Pastel 28 × 38.2 cm
Presented by Mr. M. Newstead 1980.54

Deanery Field lies in the north-east corner of the cathedral precinct, bounded on two sides by the city walls and overlooked by the King Charles Tower. Starting in 1923, the field was excavated by Professor Robert Newstead, the first Curator of the Grosvenor Museum, who discovered the remains of Roman barrack blocks. Packed within the fortress wall of Roman Chester were more than sixty long barrack blocks, each housing a century of eighty men and their centurion. The barracks in Deanery Field were fed from cookhouses situated inside the northern wall.

158

159

LOUISE RAYNER (1832-1924)

St Werburgh's Mount, St Werburgh Street, 1873

Watercolour with bodycolour
40.9 × 56.7 cm
Presented by Miss M. Newboult
1978.99

St Werburgh's Mount stood opposite the south transept of the cathedral. The house's last occupant was Thomas Hughes, author of *The Stranger's Handbook to Chester*, the city's best Victorian guide. He commissioned Louise Rayner to paint two watercolour views of his home just before it was demolished. The present St Werburgh's Mount, a group of shops behind a street-level arcade, was built in 1873-4 to the design of John Douglas. Douglas's first building in this street, St Werburgh Chambers of 1872-3, may be seen to the right of the old house.

160

WILLIAM ROBERT WRIGHT BOYD (1877-1963)

Interior of the King's Arms Kitchen, 1941

Pencil, pen & Indian ink with bodycolour 33.5 × 48.6 cm
Purchased 1982.34

The Honourable Incorporation of the King's Arms Kitchen was a gentlemen's club which met in the 'Mayor's Parlour' seen here. Dating from *c.*1770, it was a mock Corporation, probably established in opposition to Chester Corporation after a dispute over whether the mayor should be elected by the aldermen or freemen. The Honourable Incorporation lapsed after 1897 due to lack of interest, but the 'Mayor's Parlour' continued in use as a room within the *King's Arms Kitchen* public house, which was behind the Midland Bank in Eastgate Street. Transferred to the Grosvenor Museum in 1979, the room is now a café.

161

GEOFFREY APPLETON

Royal Bank of Scotland, Foregate Street, 1995

Bodycolour 41.9 × 29.6 cm
Commissioned 1995.512

This is the finest half-timbered building in Chester to be erected since the First World War. Built in 1921 by Francis Jones for the Manchester and District Bank, and extended in 1964 by Saxon Smith and Partners, it now houses the Royal Bank of Scotland. The elaborate black-and-white exterior covers a steel frame. There is a single gable to Foregate Street but three on the Frodsham Street façade, and each part of the building is slightly angled to increase its scenic effect. Inside, the banking hall rises through two storeys and has sandstone walls and a wooden balcony.

161

60

Royal Bank of Scotland

162

WILLIAM TASKER (1808-52)

Foregate Street, Looking East, 1836

Grey wash 25.6 × 34.6 cm
Purchased with grant-aid from the
V&A Purchase Grant Fund, the
National Art Collections Fund,
Arrowcroft and Lloyd's Bank 1980.69

Foregate Street is the street 'before' or
'outside' the Eastgate. It follows the
line of the main Roman road to York,
which ran through a *vicus* or civilian
settlement outside the Roman fortress.
It was also a busy street in the 17th-
19th centuries, being on the mail coach
route to London. The *Blossoms Hotel* on
the corner of St John Street was a

coaching inn of *c.*1650 which catered
for passengers as they waited for ships
to Ireland: it was rebuilt by Thomas
Meakin Lockwood in 1896. *Ye Olde
Bear's Paw*, a public house on the corner
of Frodsham Street, was demolished
in the 1950s.

162

163

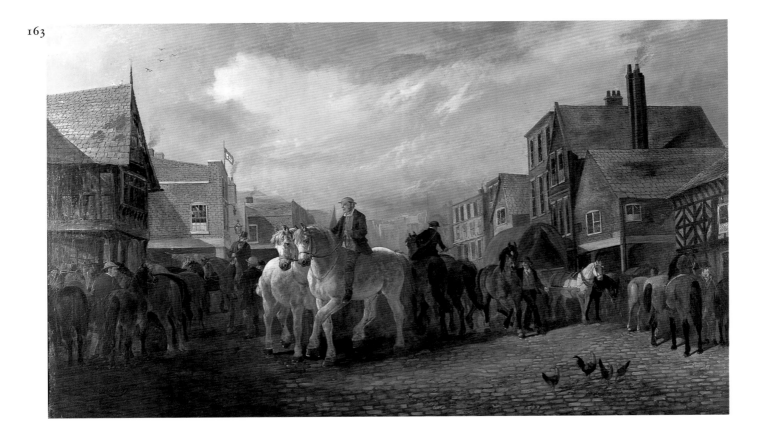

163

HENRY CHARLES WOOLLETT
(ACTIVE 1860-81)

*Chester Horse Fair, Foregate
Street, 1877*

Oil on canvas 74.7 × 125.9 cm
Presented by Horace Webber 1966.22

This view, looking west down Foregate
Street, is taken from its junction with
Love Street. Until the late 19th century **164**
this area was one of the most crowded
in Chester, with residential courtyards
and passages leading off both sides of
Foregate Street. These slum areas have
since been removed, and the street is
now commercial rather than residential. The timber-framed building on the
left, with its upper storey overhanging
the pavement and supported on timber
columns, is dated 1571 but looks mid-
17th century. The timber-framed
building on the opposite side, which
also survives today, is of roughly the
same date.

164

JOHN HAYDN JONES

*The Nine Houses, Park Street,
1995*

Watercolour over pencil 33.4 × 50.7 cm
Commissioned 1995.517 **165**

Six of the Nine Houses survive. Built
in the mid-17th century as almshouses,
residents had to be over 65 years old
and abstain from tobacco and alcohol.
Each house has a gable spanning the
timber-framed upper storey, which is
jettied over the sandstone ground
floor. This is unusual in Chester, where
the ground floors of the old buildings
beyond the Rows tend to have timber-
framing on sandstone plinths. At the
north end of this terrace is a house of
1881 by W.H. Kelly. Like many
examples of Victorian black-and-
white, it is larger and more elaborate
than the 17th-century buildings.

165

CHERYL ROBERTS

Albion Street, 1995

Watercolour over pencil 55.9 × 75.9 cm
Commissioned 1995.521

The *Albion Hotel* in Lower Bridge
Street was built as Park House in 1715
and was later known as the *Talbot Hotel*.
Its extensive pleasure grounds,
including a bowling green, extended to
Park Street. The grounds closed in
1865 and were developed with
working-class terraced housing. In the
middle of Albion Street is the
Volunteer Drill Hall, built in the
Gothic style in 1869 as the headquarters of the 2nd Volunteer Battalion
(Earl of Chester's) Cheshire Regiment.
The houses in Albion Street, built of
red brick with simple geometrical
patterns in cream-coloured brick, had
also been completed by 1869.

166

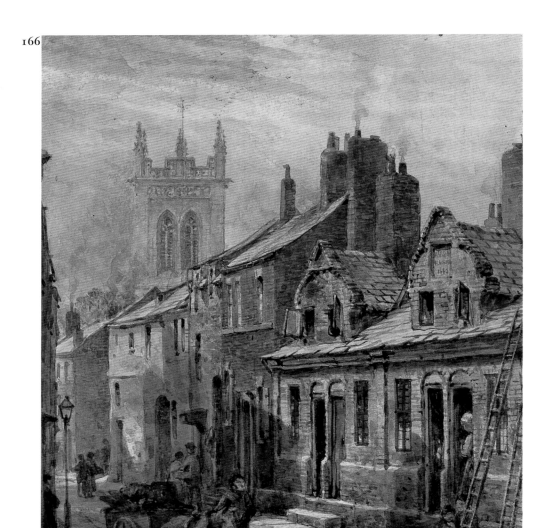

167

LOUISE RAYNER (1832-1924)

The Bear and Billet, Lower Bridge Street

Watercolour with bodycolour
26.8 ↔ 12.6 cm
Presented by T. Cann Hughes 1925.7

The *Bear and Billet*, dated 1664, is among the last of England's great timber-framed town houses. The Earls of Shrewsbury, who held half the custody of the Bridgegate at this time, built it as their town house and owned it until 1867. The bear and billet (or staff) is associated with the arms of the Earls of Warwick rather than Shrewsbury but, as a name for this inn, dates from the 18th century. The building's continuous window bands and richly-carved timbers are typical of Chester. In the gable there are doors through which grain was hoisted for storage in the attic.

168

LOUISE RAYNER (1832-1924)

The Old Edgar, Lower Bridge Street

Watercolour with bodycolour
26.8 ↔ 12.6 cm
Presented by Miss C. Cann Hughes 1950.716

Just above the *Bear and Billet*, on the corner of Shipgate Street, is the *Old Edgar*. Probably dating from the late 16th century, it has been much restored and altered, and part of its timber-framing has been replaced by brick. Formerly an inn, it is now two houses. It is named after King Edgar of England who, according to tradition, visited Chester in 973 and was rowed on the river Dee by eight subject kings in token of submission to him. This episode is depicted on the large inn sign.

166

LOUISE RAYNER (1832-1924)

Harvie's Almshouses, Duke Street

Watercolour with bodycolour
25.2 × 17.9 cm
Presented by T. Cann Hughes 1925.5

This terrace of six almshouses (of which only four are visible here) stood on the north side of Duke Street. They were built by Alderman Robert Harvie in 1692 and, as with many British buildings of this period, showed the influence of Dutch architecture. They were demolished shortly after 1892. The tower of St Mary-on-the-Hill, visible in the distance, has been moved forward slightly by the artist to improve the composition.

169

169

LOUISE RAYNER (1832-1924)

Lower Bridge Street, Looking South

Watercolour with bodycolour
22.1 × 28.2 cm
Presented by Miss B. Cann Hughes
1950.720

The east side of Lower Bridge Street between St Olave's Church and Duke Street was known as Old Coach Row. There were steps between the changes in level as it descended steeply southward, earning it the nickname 'Rotten Row'. Some of the buildings had the characteristics of a true Row, with a covered gallery above cellars entered from the street, whilst others had merely an arcade over a raised pavement. Little of the true Row buildings survived by 1880, and by 1945 the site combined conventional frontages with elements of street-level arcading. A huge garage, built for the Grosvenor Motor Company in 1962, now occupies the site.

170

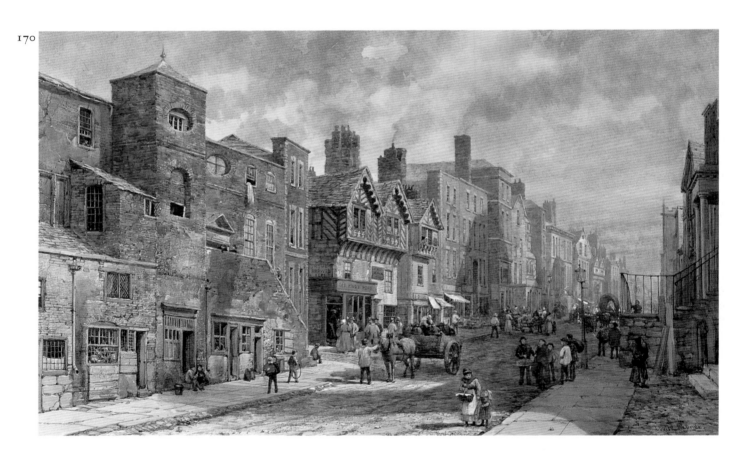

170

Louise Rayner (1832–1924)

Lower Bridge Street, Looking North

Watercolour with bodycolour
37.1 × 60.1 cm
Presented by Mrs. A. Mabel Irwin
1975.254

On the left of this picture is Gamul House. Its brick façade of *c.*1700, with oval upper windows, conceals a Jacobean timber-framed structure, but the tower seen here no longer exists. It was the home of Sir Francis Gamul, who entertained King Charles I here in 1645. A little further up is the *Old King's Head*, its top storey timber-framed, with some herringbone bracing and coving below two of the three gables. It was rebuilt or enlarged in the early 17th century as the home of Randle Holme I, the first of four generations of armorial painters and antiquaries.

171

Louise Rayner (1832–1924)

Hawarden Castle Entry, Lower Bridge Street

Watercolour with bodycolour
26.9 × 12.4 cm
Presented 1965.187

Hawarden Castle Entry, to the south of Tudor House, was a narrow passage and small court of dense and insanitary housing. The Row through Tudor House had long since been enclosed but this picture shows how, in the late 19th century, the Row walkway still joined the next building. Today the Row has gone, but timberwork survives on both sides of the opening to mark where it crossed the passage. As with many of her watercolours of Chester, Louise Rayner has captured the surface textures, with the remains of whitewash and crumbling plaster on the bricks between the timber-framing.

171

172

ALFRED BENNETT BAMFORD
(1857-1939)

*Tudor House, Lower Bridge
Street, 1929*

Watercolour over pencil 34.1 × 22.6 cm
Presented by Chester College of Further
Education 1965.180

Tudor House is dated 1503, but 1603 is
a much more likely date. The building
is timber-framed, with distinctive ogee
herringbone bracing in the two storeys
beneath the gable. The first floor is
faced with brick and has sash windows,
because the Row which originally ran
through the building was enclosed in
the early 18th century. It is interesting
to note that Alfred Bennett Bamford's
watercolours of the 1920s and '30s
show Chester's timber-framed
buildings to have been brown and
cream rather than black and white,
which is the colour-scheme of the
majority today.

173

ANN KENNEDY

20 & 22 Castle Street, 1995

Watercolour over pencil 37.6 × 55.9 cm
Commissioned 1995.519

The house on the right, no.20, was
built c.1680 for Edmund Swetenham II
of Somerford Booths near Congleton,
and its staircase with 'barleysugar'
banisters dates from this time. In 1714
it was inherited by Edmund
Swetenham III, who created an
impressive first-floor drawing room
and refaced the frontage. The house
passed to the Comberbach family, and
then to the Grosvenors, who leased it
to a succession of tenants before it
was purchased by the City Council in
1931. Forming part of the Grosvenor
Museum since 1955, no.20 is now
displayed as a sequence of nine period
rooms ranging from 1680-1925, while
no.22 serves as offices for Chester
Archaeology.

174

ALISTER WINTER ROBERTS

*The Grosvenor Museum,
Grosvenor Street, 1995*

Watercolour over pencil 42 × 72.2 cm
Commissioned 1995.520

Designed by Thomas Meakin
Lockwood, the Grosvenor Museum
was built in 1885-6 to house the
collections of the Chester Archaeological Society and the Chester Society
of Natural Science, Literature and Art,
together with Schools of Science and
Art. The Museum is named after Hugh
Lupus Grosvenor, 1st Duke of
Westminster, who donated a portion
of the site and part of the building
costs. Built of red brick with sandstone dressings in a free Renaissance
style, the reclining female figures in the
spandrels of the portal represent
Science and Art, whilst the Dutch
gables are carved with peacocks and
flanked by the talbot supporters of the
Grosvenor arms.

173

174

175

176

Neale T. Evans

4-28 Nicholas Street, 1995

Watercolour over pencil 74.3 × 55.9 cm
Commissioned 1995.525

The terrace on the west side of
Nicholas Street was designed by
Joseph Turner and built in 1781. The
identical three-storey houses with
basements are built of brick with stone
dressings, their only architectural
ornament being the door surrounds. It
is the longest and most uniform
terrace in Chester. These houses were
known as Pill-Box Promenade in the
19th century because many of them
were occupied by doctors, but most
are used as offices today. The Georgian
houses on the opposite side of
Nicholas Street were demolished in the
early 1960s when it was widened to
form the inner ring road.

175

Alfred Bennett Bamford
(1857-1939)

No. 1 White Friars, 1930

Watercolour over pencil 32.9 × 23.8 cm
Presented by Chester College of Further
Education 1965.179

The street is named after the Carmelite
friars, who wore a white mantle. Their
house in Chester was founded in the
1280s and was dissolved in 1538. No.1
White Friars is one of the least-known
genuine timber-framed houses of
Chester. The left-hand gable is dated
1658 and that on the right now bears
the date 1987, when the building was
last restored. The jettied first floor
overhangs the pavement. The long
band of first-floor windows also
projects, and is supported by carved
corbels. The left-hand gable and the
panel infills between the timbers are
decorated with moulded plasterwork,
known as pargeting.

176

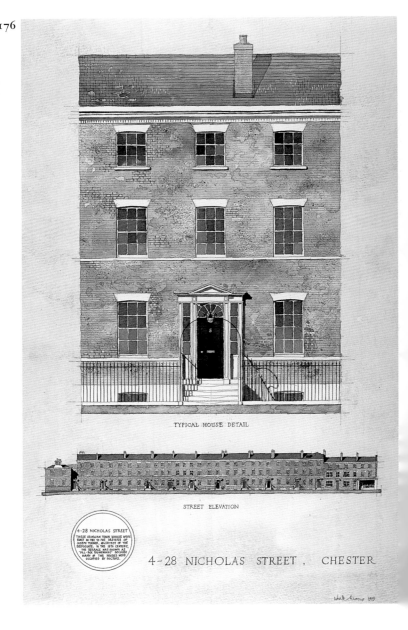

TYPICAL HOUSE DETAIL

STREET ELEVATION

4-28 NICHOLAS STREET, CHESTER

177

JOHN SKINNER PROUT (1806-76)

Stanley Palace, Watergate Street

Watercolour 37 × 25.6 cm
Purchased with grant-aid from the
Grosvenor Museum Society 1985.9

Stanley Palace was built in 1591 for Sir
Peter Warburton of Grafton, Vice-
Chamberlain of the Chester Exchequer and M.P. for the City. On his death
in 1621 it passed to his son-in-law Sir
Thomas Stanley of Alderley, a kinsman
of the Earls of Derby. By the mid-
19th century it was threatened with
demolition, and reconstruction in the
United States was suggested. It was
purchased by the Chester Archaeological Society, who sold it in 1889 to the
Earl of Derby. In 1929 Stanley Palace
was given by the Earl of Derby to
Chester Corporation, which heavily
restored it in 1935.

178

TOM MORTON

*Watergate House, Watergate
Street, 1995*

Watercolour 35.5 × 53.9 cm
Commissioned 1995.523

Watergate House was designed by
Thomas Harrison and built in 1820 for
Henry Potts, Clerk of the Peace for the
County of Cheshire. Constructed of
brick with stone dressings, it is the only
example of a town house by Harrison.
His villas were usually stuccoed, but
brick may have been chosen to fit in
with the existing houses in Watergate
Street. The front door, flanked by
Ionic columns and pilasters, is placed
in the recessed
and curved corner of the house.
Inside, the entrance leads, on a
diagonal axis, to an oval vestibule,
followed by a top-lit central hall.

Chester - Watergate House   Tom Morton 1995

179

179

CHARLES GINNER (1878-1952)

'The Lock Gates', 1933

Oil on canvas 67.6 × 49.6 cm
Purchased with grant-aid from the
MGC/V&A Purchase Grant Fund and
the Pilgrim Trust 1991.232

This bridge carries South View Road
over the Shropshire Union Canal. In
the foreground is the Dee Basin, which
leads to the River Dee. Beyond the
lock is Tower Wharf, where the canal
to Ellesmere Port begins. The two
chimneys in the distance, now
demolished, belonged to a steam saw
mill which supplied timber for the
boatbuilding yard beside the canal. The
Chester Canal was inaugurated in 1772
and became part of the Shropshire
Union in 1842. Chester was a thriving
canal port throughout the 19th
century, and the canal traffic continued
between the Wars, with oil products
and metal forming the main cargoes.

180

180

HENRY WYATT (1794-1840)

Telford's Warehouse, Raymond Street

Pencil 11 × 18.1 cm
Presented by Mr. Wiltmore Taylor
1951.43(6)

Tower Wharf, at the junction of the
two canals, opened in 1797 and retains
an important group of canal buildings.
The large brick building in this picture
is now a restaurant known as Telford's
Warehouse. Built by Thomas Telford,
the canal company's engineer, it was
constructed over the canal to allow
boats to be loaded or unloaded directly
beneath it—a practical design typical
of Telford. The canal company's
headquarters, now Diocesan House,
were built beside it in *c.*1815. This view
is taken from the Northgate Locks,
originally five locks but now three,
hewn out of the sandstone in 1779.

181

181

RICHARD HORE

*Exterior View of General
Railway Station, 1996*

Pencil 38 × 55 cm
Commissioned 1996.100

The first railways came to Chester in
1840, when lines to Birkenhead and
Crewe were opened, and four further
lines were opened between 1846 and
1850. From 1840-8 a temporary station
was used to the north of the present
General Station, which was built in
1847-8. It was designed by Francis
Thompson and built by the great
Cheshire-born railway engineer
Thomas Brassey. Constructed of brick
with stone dressings in the Italianate
style, it is one of Britain's most
splendid early railway stations. Its
façade, measuring a quarter of a mile,
is one of the longest in Europe.

182

JOHN GRESTY (ACTIVE 1850-82)
Interior of General Railway Station

Lithograph 21 × 27.3 cm
Presented by Miss D.H. & Miss E.M. Mayers 1957.78

This picture shows the interior of the newly-constructed station. Its two elegant iron roofs, each spanning 60 feet, were designed by C.H. Wild. In the centre of the general departure platform stood the manager's office, overlooking the passengers. To the right were the refreshment and waiting rooms, with the offices of the railway companies above them. Chester also had a second railway station, the Northgate Station, from 1874-1969, where the Northgate Arena leisure centre now stands.

183

184

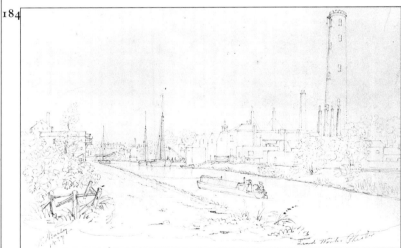

183

John Henry Metcalfe (active 1869) after John Douglas (1830-1911)

Triumphal Arch, City Road, 1869

Lithograph 37.8 × 25.4 cm
Presented by the Revd. Canon Maurice Ridgway 1955.73

City Road was laid out in the early 1860s as a highway from the General Station to Foregate Street. Where City Road crosses the Shropshire Union Canal, this triumphal arch was erected for the visit of the Prince of Wales (later King Edward VII) to open Chester Town Hall on 15 October 1869. Designed by John Douglas, it was a temporary structure with painted-on black-and-white timbering. Its roofscape combined many of Douglas's favourite Germanic features, with its projecting turrets, steeply hipped roofs, miniature dormers and bold finials, and the Chester press likened the arch to one of the gateways of Prague.

184

Thomas Bailey (active 1828-64)

Chester Leadworks, 1837

Pencil 22 × 30 cm
Presented by Alderman E. Peter Jones 1943.330(46)

The Chester Leadworks, on the north bank of the canal, were established by Walker, Parker & Co. to produce red and white lead and lead shot. The circular brick shot tower, 168 feet tall, was built in 1799. To produce lead shot, molten lead was mixed with arsenic to make it form hard, spherical globules. It was then poured through a mesh at the top of the tower. Droplets of molten lead solidified as pellets as they fell down into a tank of cold water at the bottom. Very few shot towers have survived, and Chester's is the best preserved of its date.

185

George Pickering (1794-1857)

The Rock Garden at Hoole House

Watercolour with bodycolour over pencil 39.2 × 57.2 cm
Purchased 1960.168

Hoole House, two miles from the centre of Chester, was built in 1760 for William Hamilton. From 1815-57 it was the residence of Lady Elizabeth Broughton. Thomas Harrison extended the house for her, and she created a remarkable rock garden. Beyond the flower garden rose tall and jagged heaps of rock, up to 34 feet high and covered with alpine plants. The design of the rockwork was modelled on the mountains of Savoy and the Chamonix valley, complete with fragments of white marble simulating snow and a glacier of spar. Hoole House was demolished in 1972 and new housing was built on the site.

186

Luci Melegari

Grosvenor Park, 1995

Collograph 50.1 × 50.6 cm
Commissioned 1995.526

Grosvenor Park was laid out in 1865-7 and presented to the city by Richard Grosvenor, 2nd Marquess of Westminster. The landscape, covering about 20 acres, was planned by Sir Joseph Paxton's pupil Edward Kemp. The architectural features were designed by John Douglas and include the entrance lodge and a canopy over a spring known as Billy Hobby's Well. The white marble statue of the 2nd Marquess in Garter robes, by Thomas Thorneycroft, was erected in 1869 at the junction of four avenues. Three arches from the Shipgate, St Michael's Church and St Mary's Nunnery were re-erected in the park, which still retains much of its Victorian character.

187

Brian Gorman

Forest House, Love Street, 1995

Acrylic & graphite 68.4 × 44.5 cm
Commissioned 1995.524

Built *c.*1780 as the town house of the Barnstons of Crewe Hill, Forest House was the grandest house in Georgian Chester. The surviving central block is three bays wide and three storeys high, with a rusticated ground floor and a pedimented gable. Colonel Roger Barnston died in 1837, and by 1856 the house had become auction rooms. It became a furniture depository *c.*1875, and today houses a nightclub. Forest House originally had a transverse oval forecourt opening onto Foregate Street, but this was replaced by the Co-operative Stores in 1904. Forest Street and the Love Street School of 1909 occupy the site of its garden.

188

Moses Griffith (1747-1819)

St John's Church and the Groves

Pen and ink with watercolour
25.5 × 40.7 cm
Presented by the National Art
Collections Fund 1960.64

At the far left is the back of Dee
House, built in 1730 over the south-
west quarter of the Roman amphitheatre. The large red-brick house
facing the river was begun before 1745
for Bishop Peploe, and the canted bay
and the wing behind it were added a
little later. From the 1870s until 1921
this house was the palace of the
bishops of Chester. The large house
with the central bow window was built
in the 1780s and demolished some
time between 1862-74, but St John's
Cottage, behind it to the right, still
survives. Behind that rises the great
west tower of St John's Church.

189

AFTER WILSON (LATE 19TH/EARLY 20TH CENTURY)

Queen's Park Suspension Bridge and the Groves

Photogravure 13.7 × 18.9 cm
Purchased 1979.13

The Groves are a tree-lined riverside promenade on the north bank of the Dee. The central section, seen in the previous picture, was originally laid out by Charles Croughton in 1725, and the western end was laid out in 1880-1 at the expense of Alderman Charles Brown. There are landing stages for pleasure boats giving cruises up the Dee, and rowing boats and small motor boats can also be hired. The Groves continue eastward beyond the Queen's Park Suspension Bridge, which was built in 1852 and rebuilt in 1923. This links Chester with Queen's Park, a villa estate laid out by James Harrison in the 1850s.

190

WILLIAM MONK (1863-1937)

Skating on the River Dee, 1890

Etching 17.4 × 24.7 cm
Presented by P.H. Woodmansey
1993.90

Skating on the Dee was a popular pastime on the rare occasions when the river froze. To the right of the weir is the floating swimming bath, which had replaced the public baths established in 1849 outside the north-west corner of the city walls. The floating bath, run by the Corporation, was only in use during the summer months. During a flood in 1898 it broke from its moorings and became stranded on top of the weir. It was replaced in position, but did not survive long after the opening of the new public baths in Union Street in 1901.

191

UNKNOWN ARTIST (ACTIVE 1851)

Dee Mills, 1851

Pencil 17.6 × 25.6 cm
Presented by T. Cann Hughes 1925.3

The weir is thought to have been built under Hugh Lupus, Earl of Chester (d.1101), in order to provide power for a water mill. Since all citizens were obliged to have their corn ground there, the mill was highly profitable. It belonged to the earl, who let it out to individuals for a high annual payment; the lessees kept the fees for grinding and became notorious for their extortion. The Wrench family purchased the mills from the Crown in the late 18th century and operated them until acquired by the Corporation in 1895. Having been burned, repaired and enlarged several times, they were finally demolished in 1910.

192

191

MARK COOK (1868-*c.*1934)

Old Dee Bridge at Dusk

Oil on board 22 × 27 cm
Bequeathed by Councillor S.H.M.
Lloyd 1989.122

A wooden bridge existed across the
Dee at this point from at least the early
13th century, but was destroyed by
floods on several occasions. In 1387
the city was given permission to
rebuild the bridge in stone, and the
Handbridge end of the bridge was
again rebuilt at the end of the 15th
century. A gate at that end was
demolished in the 1780s, and the
bridge was widened on the east side in
1825-6 by the construction of a
footway. At the city end of the bridge,
to the left of the picture, is the hydro-
electric power station, built in 1913 on
the site of the Dee Mills.

192

193

T. CATHERALL (ACTIVE 1856-80) AFTER
JOHN MUSGROVE (ACTIVE 1810-31)

The Minerva Shrine, 1829

Etching 22.5 × 30.4 cm
1965.264

The sandstone outcrops to the south
of the river provided an easily
accessible quarry for the vast amounts
of stone required to build the Roman
fortress. Carved into the face of one
of these outcrops, situated in what is
now known as Edgar's Field, is an
image of Minerva, the Roman goddess
of warriors and craftsmen. No other
shrine like this survives in its original
location. The image has weathered, so
that now only a faint outline remains:
Minerva was originally depicted with
an owl, helmet, spear and shield.
Offerings may have been placed on the
altar by the left pillar.

ROMAN ANTIQUE

194

J. ELLIS (LATE 19TH CENTURY)

Handbridge

Oil on canvas 55.4 × 86 cm
1996.569

In the 19th century the suburb of
Handbridge, south of the river Dee,
was an industrial area with working-
class housing. Shown in the foreground is Greenway Street, where the
Dee salmon fishermen lived. Their
boats are drawn up to the river bank,
with their net drying stakes to the
right. Many of the cottages were
rebuilt after the Second World War.

Behind is the church of St Mary-
without-the-Walls with its soaring
spire, designed by F.B. Wade for the 1st
Duke of Westminster and built in
1885-7. The large house to the right is
Handbridge Rectory, designed by G.E.
Grayson and E.A. Ould.

195

EVANS & GRESTY (ACTIVE 1854-60)

Chester Cemetery, Overleigh

Engraving 8.2 × 11.5 cm
Presented by Mrs. Bradbury
1973.32(m)

The cemetery was laid out in 1848-50
for the Chester General Cemetery
Company by a Mr. Lister, and the
buildings were designed by Thomas
Mainwaring Penson. The highly
picturesque layout, with trees and
shrubs, winding footpaths and a lake
with swans, is an early example of the
park-like burial grounds favoured by
the Victorians. This westward view
shows the Nonconformist chapel
beside the lake, the circular temple of
the Turner monument to the right, and
the Anglican chapel in the Norman
style on the high ground. A great
variety of Victorian monuments
remain, but all the buildings and the
lake have gone.

196

THOMAS BAILEY (ACTIVE 1828-64)

*The Grosvenor Lodge, Overleigh,
1837*

Pencil 22.7 × 29.5 cm
Presented by Alderman E. Peter Jones
1943.330(17)

The Grosvenor Lodge was built in
1835 for the 1st Marquess of Westminster. Situated near the southern end of
the new Grosvenor Bridge, it commanded the principal approach to
Eaton Hall from Chester. It was the
most celebrated work of Thomas
Jones, and was based on the gateway
of St Augustine's Abbey at Canterbury.
Eaton Hall, the seat of the
Grosvenors, was at this time a
spectacular Gothic Revival mansion,
rebuilt by William Porden in 1803-12
with wings added by Benjamin
Gummow in 1823-5. Eaton Hall was
subsequently remodelled or rebuilt
four times, and the Grosvenor Lodge
was replaced by the present Overleigh
Lodge *c.*1893.

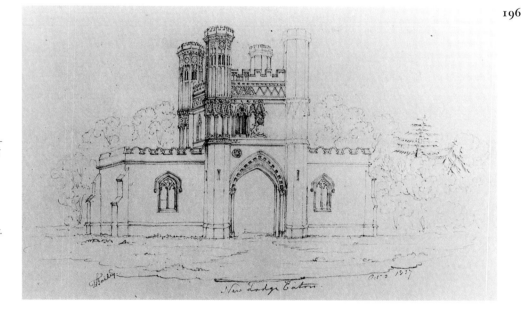

New Lodge Eaton

THOMAS BAILEY (ACTIVE 1828-64)

Grosvenor Bridge under construction, 1831

Pencil 17.5 × 26.4 cm
Presented by Alderman E. Peter Jones
1943.330(44)

The Grosvenor Bridge was designed by Thomas Harrison, whose first plans were made in 1818. There were numerous changes before a single span masonry arch was approved in 1826, and the foundation stone was laid by the 2nd Earl Grosvenor in 1827. The contractor was James Trubshaw, working under the supervision of Harrison's pupil William Cole junior, with Jesse Hartley as clerk of works. The abutments, founded on rock, were completed in 1829. The massive centring, designed by Trubshaw, was erected in 1830. It consisted of struts radiating from the tops of temporary stone piers, braced horizontally in both directions and supporting planks bent to the curve of the arch.

198

LOUIS HAGHE (1806-95) AFTER
THOMAS BAILEY (ACTIVE 1828-64)

Grosvenor Bridge

Lithograph 19.8 × 24.8 cm
Purchased 1979.22

Thomas Harrison died in 1829, the bridge was formally opened by Princess Victoria in 1831, and it was completed in 1833. The Grosvenor Bridge is Harrison's greatest work of engineering: at 200 feet it was the longest single span stone arch in the world until 1864. The outer courses of the arch and the quoins are of Anglesey limestone, while the rest of the bridge is cased in Peckforton sandstone. The great segmental arch springs from the base of the abutments, which have niches and carry pediments above a Doric frieze. At either end, a semicircular arch links the bridge with the embankments which carry the approach roads.

199

WILLIAM TASKER (1808-52)

'Millipede' on the Roodee, 1843

Oil on canvas 62.2 × 78.6 cm
Purchased with grant-aid from the V&A Purchase Grant Fund, the National Art Collections Fund and the Pilgrim Trust 1980.32

'Roodee' means 'Rood island', and it seems probable that there was a cross (or 'rood') on an island in the Dee, which once flowed beside the western city wall. Organised horse-racing on the Roodee began in 1540. The races were held on Shrove Tuesday until 1609, when the date was changed to St George's Day. In the 18th century the races took place during the first week of May and became a major social event. Race meetings are now held five times a year on the Roodee. 'Millipede' won the Chester Tradesmen's Cup in 1843, a race introduced in 1824, which became the Chester Cup in 1893.

200

JOHN MCGAHEY (ACTIVE 1845-70)

The Royal Agricultural Show on the Roodee, 1858

Chromolithograph 23 × 38.8 cm
Presented by W. S. Jones 1962.11

In addition to horse-racing, the Roodee has been used for a range of events requiring a large open space, including military reviews. This picture records the Royal Agricultural Show which was held here in June 1858. The view is taken from the city walls, and shows the back of the first grandstand built in 1817. Enlarged several times later in the 19th century, it was rebuilt in 1899-1900, and was rebuilt again in 1985-8 after a fire. Skirting the far edge of the Roodee is the railway viaduct and its bridge over the Dee, which opened in 1846.

END

BIBLIOGRAPHY

BOOKS

Addleshaw, G.W.O., *Chester Cathedral* (1975)

Anon., *A History of the Municipal Charities of Chester from 1837 to 1875* (1875)

Bevan, R.M., *The Roodee* (1989)

Boughton, P.J., 'Cheshire', *Blue Guide: Churches and Chapels of Northern England* (1991)

Braun, G. & Hogenberg, F., *Civitates Orbis Terrarum*, vol.I, parts 1/2 (reprint 1966)

Buckler, J. & J.C., *Views of Eaton Hall* (1826)

Colvin, H., *A Biographical Dictionary of British Architects 1600-1840*, 2nd edn. (1978)

Glass, J.V.S. & Patrick, J.M., *The Royal Chester Rowing Club Centenary History* (1939)

Harris, B., *Chester* (1979)

Hemingway, J., *History of the City of Chester*, 2 vols. (1831)

Hubbard, E., *The Work of John Douglas* (1991)

Hughes, T., *The Stranger's Handbook to Chester* (1856)

Hughes, T., *Ancient Chester: Twenty-Nine Etchings by Batenham and Musgrove* (1880)

Kennett, A.M. (ed.), *Loyal Chester: A brief history of Chester in the Civil War period* (1984)

King, D., *The Vale Royal of England or The County Palatine of Chester* (reprint 1972)

Montagu, J., *Roman Baroque Sculpture: The Industry of Art* (1992)

Morriss, R. & Hoverd, K., *The Buildings of Chester* (1993)

Ockrim, M.A.R., 'The Life and Work of Thomas Harrison of Chester 1744-1829' (unpublished PhD thesis, University of London, Courtauld Institute of Art, 1988)

Ormerod, G., *History of Cheshire*, 3 vols., 2nd edn. (1882)

Pace, P., *The Architecture of George Pace* (1990)

Pevsner, N. & Hubbard, E., *Cheshire* (1971)

Smalley, S.S., *Chester Cathedral* (1989)

Swift, R. (ed.), *Victorian Chester* (1996)

Ward, T.E., *Chester Observed* (1982)

Ward, T.E., *Memories of Yesterday* (1983)

Ward, T.E., *Chester in Camera* (1985)

PAMPHLETS

Cheshire County Council, *A Chester Church Trail* (1989)

Cheshire County Council, *Chester Walls Walk* (1992)

Chester City Council, *Heritage Walk 1* (1975)

Chester City Council, *Heritage Walk 2* (1977)

Chester City Council, *Heritage Walk 3* (1979)

Chester City Council, *Minerva Shrine* (1992)

Chester Civic Trust, *Chester Cemetery, Overleigh* (1994)

Harris, B.E., *The Church and Parish of St Michael, Chester* (1981)

Willshaw, E., 'The Rows of Chester' (unpublished)

Wordplay Publishing, *Roman Chester* (1994)

Wordplay Publishing, *The Unique Chester Rows* (1995)

Wordplay Publishing, *Chester Cathedral: The Secret Past* (1996)

INDEX OF ARTISTS

INDEX OF ARCHITECTS

Lockwood, Philip H., 154
Lockwood, Thomas Meakin, 121, 124,
    135, 140, 148, 162, 174
Lockwood, W.T., 142
Luxton, David, 154
Lyell, Michael, Associates, 152
Lynn, William Henry, of Belfast, 151

Ould, E.A., Grayson, G.E., &, 145, 194

Pace, George, 20, 31
Parkes, E. Mainwaring, 118
Paxton, Sir Joseph, 186

Penson, Thomas Mainwaring, 48, 137,
    195
Porden, William, 196

Richard of Chester, 18

Saxon Smith & Partners, 161
Scott, George Gilbert, junior, 16
Scott, Sir George Gilbert, 15, 19, 23,
    24, 26, 28, 30, 31
Scott, Sir Giles Gilbert, 37, 38
Seddon, John Pollard, 56
Strong, James, 131, 156

Tapper, Sir Walter & Michael, 97
Taylor, Sir Robert, 23
Telford, Thomas, 180
Thompson, Francis, 181
Trubshaw, James, 197
Turner, Joseph, 96, 176

Wade, F.B., 194
Weedon, Harry, 155
Wild, C.H., 182

INDEX OF PLACES

Numbers refer to illustrations

Abbey Gateway, 42
Abbey Square, 22, 41
Addleshaw Tower, 20
Agricola Tower - see Castle
Albion Hotel, 165
Albion Street, 165
Amphitheatre, 97, 188
Anchorite's Cell, 64
Assembly Room, 128

Barclay's Bank, 22
Barn Lane, 157
Bars, The, 2
Baths, 190
Bath Street, 68
Bear and Billet, 96, 167, 168
Beaverbrooks, 137
Billy Hobby's Well, 186
Bishop Lloyd's Palace, 124-126
Bishop's Palace, 22, 23, 41, 188
Blacon, 63
Blossoms Hotel, 162
Blue Bell Inn, 132
Bluecoat School, 12, 65, 83
Bolland's, 137
Bonewaldesthorne's Tower, 89, 91, 92
Booth Mansion, 128
Boughton, 6, 7, 67
Bridgegate, 4-6, 94-96, 117, 167
Bridge House, 144
Bridge of Sighs, 83
Bridge Street & Row, 53, 57, 60, 61,
    121, 139-143, 147, 148
Broken Shin Row, 133
Buttershops, 135

Canal, 21, 74, 79, 82, 179, 180, 183, 184
Castle, 5, 6, 11, 54, 73, 99-118
Castle Drive, 117
Castle Street, 173
Cathedral, 4-7, 12-42, 79, 111, 157-159
Cattle Market, 10
Cemetery, 10, 195
Christleton, 37
City Club, 149
City Road, 71, 183
City Walls, 1-5, 10, 73-98, 158, 190
College, 66
Commerce House, 12
Commercial Coffee Room & News
    Room, 149

Commercial Hall, 10
Common Hall, 58
Congregational Church, 8
Co-operative Stores, 187
County Hall, 118
Cow Lane, 21
Cow Lane Bridge, 21
Crane Wharf, 10
Cross, 60, 121, 128, 129, 139, 140
Curzon Park, 10

Dark Row or Lofts, 134-136
Deanery Field, 158
Dee Basin, 10, 179
Dee House, 188
Dee Mills, 10, 96, 114, 191, 192
Deva Hotel, 129
Deva Terrace, 11
Dill's Tower, 87, 88
Diocesan House, 180
Dublin Packet, 130
Duke Street, 166, 169
Dutch Houses, 148

Earl's Eye, 7, 11
Eastgate, 3, 75-78, 137, 162
Eastgate Street & Row, 77, 120, 121,
    133-138, 140, 160
Eaton Hall, 196
Edgar's Field, 193
English Presbyterian Church of Wales,
    71
Exchange, 4, 5, 91, 150, 151

Falcon Inn, 145
Fire Station, 156
Fish Market, 150
Fleshmongers' Row, 125
Foregate Street, 6, 8, 10, 77, 161-163,
    183, 187
Forest House, 6, 7, 187
Forest Street, 187
Forum, 152
Frodsham Street, 10, 21, 161, 162

Gallows Hill, 1, 6
Gamul House, 170
Gasworks, 10
General Railway Station, 181-183
Gloverstone, 104
Goblin Tower, 87, 88

God's Providence House, 122, 129
Gorse Stacks, 10
Green Market, 150
Greenway Street, 194
Grosvenor Bridge, 10, 196-198
Grosvenor Hotel, 137
Grosvenor Lodge, 196
Grosvenor Motor Company, 169
Grosvenor Museum, 81, 158, 160, 173,
    174
Grosvenor Park, 94, 108, 186
Grosvenor Park Baptist Chapel, 69
Grosvenor Park Road, 68, 69
Grosvenor Precinct, 137, 142
Grosvenor Road, 117
Grosvenor Street, 53, 54
Groves, The, 11, 22, 64, 188, 189
Guildhall - see Holy Trinity Church

Habitat, 70
Handbridge, 1, 5, 10, 114, 192, 194
Handbridge Rectory, 194
Harvie's Almshouses, 166
Hawarden Castle Entry, 171
Heritage Centre - see St Michael's
    Church
Hermitage, 64
Holy Trinity Church, 4-6, 12, 62, 63
Hoole House, 185
Horse Fair, 163
Hunter Street, 12, 153
Hunter's Walk, 153
Hydro-Electric Power Station, 192

Inner Ring Road, 12, 55, 86, 157

King Charles Tower, 74, 79-81, 158
King's Arms Kitchen, 160
King's Buildings, 157
King's School, 22, 38
King Street, 157

Lamb Row & Inn, 53, 119, 146
Leadworks, 184
Leche House, 123
Library, 154
Little St John's Chapel, 5, 65, 83
Little St John Street, 98
Lorimers' Row, 132
Love Street, 163, 187
Love Street School, 187